U.S. Sanitary Commission Statistical Bureau

**Ages of U. S. Volunteer Soldiery**

U.S. Sanitary Commission Statistical Bureau

**Ages of U. S. Volunteer Soldiery**

ISBN/EAN: 9783337137168

Printed in Europe, USA, Canada, Australia, Japan

Cover: Foto ©ninafisch / pixelio.de

More available books at **www.hansebooks.com**

U. S. SANITARY COMMISSION.

STATISTICAL BUREAU.

# AGES

OF

# U. S. VOLUNTEER SOLDIERY.

NEW YORK.

1866.

, DEAR SIR, —

Inclosed is my Report on the Ages of Volunteers in the late war. The general results were communicated, by permission, to the National Academy of Sciences at its session in August last, and this Report was read before the Commission in November; but the Appendix, concerning the Ages of a Population in general, has been prepared since that time.

For most of the troops comprised within the limits of the present discussion, no descriptive muster-rolls exist. The Ages, Nativities, and Statures of those troops whose descriptions are on record will soon be made the subject of another Report.

I am, dear Sir,

Very respectfully and sincerely yours,

B. A. GOULD,
*Actuary U. S. Sanitary Commission.*

JOHN S. BLATCHFORD, ESQ.,
*General Secretary U. S. Sanitary Commission.*

# CORRIGENDA.

Page 6, line 23, *for* face      *read* force.
" 10, " 19, " 28.4843    " 28.4850.
" 30, " 28, " Column 9   " Column 3.
" 39, " 24, " one million " one hundred thousand.

# AGES

OF

# UNITED STATES VOLUNTEER SOLDIERY.

---

## 1. *Introductory.*

ON taking charge of the Statistical Department of the United States Sanitary Commission, in August, 1864, it was found that considerable progress had been made in collecting the ages of the soldiers of our volunteer regiments, — an investigation which had been suggested and commenced by Mr. ELLIOTT, the accomplished and skilful statistician, who, not very long before, had relinquished the direction of this Bureau of the Commission.

Although the best use to be made of the materials appeared somewhat uncertain, it did not seem proper to discontinue inquiries already so far advanced ; and the large experience of Mr. ELLIOTT in matters connected with vital statistics gave assurance that valuable as well as interesting results were likely to be deduced from a thorough study of these data.

The collection of these materials was therefore continued and completed, by means of the muster-rolls on file at the War Department in Washington, to which access was courteously afforded by General E. D. TOWNSEND, Acting Adjutant-General, and Colonel SAMUEL BRECK, who was in charge of the rolls. Tables have thus been formed for twenty-seven States, Territories, or geographical groups, exhibiting the number of men at each year of age in the volunteer organizations, at the time of their muster into the service of the United States. The officers are tabulated as a distinct class; and the three arms of the military service — infantry, cavalry, and artillery — have been treated separately.

The original collection of the materials was principally made by Mr. T. J. O'CONNELL, until lately the efficient and accurate chief clerk of the Statistical Department, and was completed by Mr. E. A. WILSON. The tabulation has been made by Messrs. O'CONNELL, WILSON, A. A. BROOKE, and JOHN N. STOCKWELL; and the greater part of the computations has been performed by Mr. STOCKWELL alone, with great care, perseverance, and ability.

The recruits who joined these original regiments after their first organization and acceptance into the national service are not included; and the limits of the investigation have excluded all drafted men, substitutes, &c. Moreover, many regiments belonging within these limits are omitted, because organized since the collection of the data for the States to which they belong; but the number of these is comparatively small, and inadequate to exert any sensible effect upon the results. The degree of completeness may be seen by the following table, which shows the number and date of the latest regiment included in the collection.

| | | | | | | | |
|---|---|---|---|---|---|---|---|
| Arkansas | 2d Infantry, | latest. | | Mississippi | Marine Brig. | only organ'n. |
| California | 4th | " | 1862, Feb. | | Missouri | 34th Infantry | 1862, Dec. |
| Connecticut | 28th | " | 1862, Nov. | | Nevada | 1st | " | 1864, June. |
| Delaware | 2d | " | 1861, Dec. | | N. Hampshire | 18th | " | 1864, Sept. |
| Illinois | 131st | " | 1864, June. | | New Jersey | 25th | " | 1862, Sept. |
| Indiana | 115th | " | 1863, Aug. | | N. Mexico | 4th | " | 1863. |
| Iowa | 48th | " | 1865. | | New York | 177th | " | 1863, June. |
| Kansas | 15th | " | 1863. | | Ohio | 128th | " | 1863, Aug. |
| Kentucky | 52d | " | 1864. | | Pennsylvania | 155th | " | 1863, Jan. |
| Louisiana | N. O. Vols. | 1864, May. | | Rhode Island | 12th | " | 1862, Oct. |
| Maine | 28th Infantry | 1864. | | Tennessee | 8th | " | 1864. |
| Maryland | 10th | " | 1864, June. | | Vermont | 16th | " | 1862, Oct. |
| Mass. | 59th | " | 1864, July. | | W. Virginia | 15th | " | 1862, Sept. |
| Michigan | 27th | " | 1864, Aug. | | Wash. Terr. | 1st | " | only reg't. |
| Minnesota | 10th | " | 1864, Aug. | | Wisconsin | 53d | " | 1864. |

The total number of volunteers whose ages have thus been investigated is 1 049 457, of whom 1 012 273 were enlisted men, and 37 184 were commissioned officers. All except 1½ per centum (.01495) of the men, and 3⅓ per centum (.0331) of the officers, were between the ages of 18 and 46 years at the date of their enlistment or commission. Those beyond these limits have not been included in the determination of the general formulas, so that these depend upon the statistics of ages for 1 022 600 men, of whom 35 953 were commissioned officers.*

The results have proved amenable to law in a higher degree than I had ventured to anticipate. Residual discordances exist, of course, between the numbers for each year of age, as derived from the tabulated records, and those indicated by the general formulas deduced from the whole series; yet where these discordances attain any essential magnitude, they may almost invariably be made to yield instructive and useful information.

The results attained, for that portion of the population who thus rushed to the field at their country's call, naturally suggest analogous inquiries regarding the white male population of the United States, and especially relative to the population of that portion of the country which furnished the volunteers under consideration. And it was not until after many unavailing efforts to obtain information as to the distribution of our population by ages, that the great deficiency of our knowledge of the facts and laws relative to this very important subject became manifest.

The only published attempt, of which I am aware, to classify the population of the United States according to years of age is very crude, and the method pursued yields results quite at variance from the truth. The only trustworthy facts are contained in the summaries of the census-returns; and the groups into which the population is there divided are altogether too large to permit the desired laws to be deduced with ease. It is earnestly to be hoped that in future census-publications the groups may be so made as to include intervals of age not greater than five years.

It thus became important, if only for the sake of comparison between the ages of the volunteer troops and that of the population whence they sprung, to subject the census of 1860 to a similar discussion. And I cannot but think that the results elicited might be advantageously employed, so far as they apply and extend, for the life-tables of our insurance and annuity offices. The life-curve for our American population is clearly diverse from the curve on which the present English tables are based;

---

* The prescribed limits of military age at the commencement of the rebellion were 18 and 45 years; but the large proportional number at the age of 45 seems to indicate that the law was so interpreted as to permit the acceptance of volunteers whose age at their last birthday did not exceed 45 years.

and it is a source of regret that the proper limits of the present investigation forbid its extension into the tempting fields of inquiry which their comparison suggests.

The fact which first attracts attention among the results of this research is the marked diversity between the distribution of the ages of officers and that of the enlisted men. Each follows a clearly manifest law ; in each case the law is deducible with close approximation to the truth ; so also is the law governing the ages of our population ; yet each of the three is utterly different from the other two. The sources of the diversity may well be made the object of careful research, and not without a reasonable probability of useful results. Certain discordances between the recorded and the computed numbers for a few particular ages will be considered hereafter.

## 2. *Ages of the Enlisted Men.*

The grand total of the rank and file of the volunteers whose ages are included in this discussion is shown in the following tabular view, which exhibits the recorded age at last birthday for the entire number ; although, as already stated, those under 18 or over 45 (last birthday), 15 626 in all, have been excluded from the general discussion. These excluded cases represent two classes, viz. the boys, chiefly drummers, musicians, &c., and the men who, although past the legal age, were so sturdy or earnest that the enrolling officers did not, at that time of great national peril, feel justified in insisting on an absolute compliance with the legal qualifications.

In the column entitled " Miscellaneous " are included all those organizations which do not belong strictly within the three principal arms of the military service, such as Engineers, Sharpshooters, Mounted Infantry, Coast Guards, Marine Brigades, &c., together with a few regiments or battalions for which the statistics were received after the special computations for Infantry, Cavalry, and Artillery had been completed, so that their incorporation with these would have required a repetition of the calculations without producing any essential change in the result.

# TABLE I.

## *Classified Summary of Enlisted Volunteers.*

| Age at last birthday. | ACTUAL NUMBER OF MEN. | | | | Total at each year of age. |
|---|---|---|---|---|---|
| | Infantry. | Cavalry. | Artillery. | Miscellaneous. | |
| 13 | 113 | 5 | 0 | 9 | 127 |
| 14 | 288 | 15 | 2 | 25 | 330 |
| 15 | 636 | 49 | 21 | 67 | 773 |
| 16 | 2053 | 232 | 61. | 412 | 2758 |
| 17 | 4653 | 638 | 226 | 908 | 6425 |
| 18 | 103420 | 15013 | 5400 | 9642 | 133475 |
| 19 | 71226 | 9767 | 3439 | 5783 | 90215 |
| 20 | 56238 | 7864 | 2627 | 4329 | 71058 |
| 21 | 75978 | 12081 | 4416 | 4661 | 97136 |
| 22 | 57485 | 9096 | 3107 | 3703 | 73391 |
| 23 | 48954 | 7806 | 2759 | 3198 | 62717 |
| 24 | 40852 | 6361 | 2163 | 2719 | 52095 |
| 25 | 36383 | 5724 | 2012 | 2507 | 46626 |
| 26 | 31292 | 4831 | 1768 | 2352 | 40243 |
| 27 | 26369 | 4192 | 1505 | 2220 | 34286 |
| 28 | 27196 | 4318 | 1525 | 2273 | 35312 |
| 29 | 18833 | 2845 | 1087 | 1748 | 24513 |
| 30 | 21937 | 3251 | 1213 | 1959 | 28360 |
| 31 | 12814 | 2053 | 796 | 2301 | 17954 |
| 32 | 17038 | 2450 | 931 | 1548 | 21967 |
| 33 | 13678 | 1930 | 753 | 1598 | 17979 |
| 34 | 12004 | 1679 | 724 | 1333 | 15740 |
| 35 | 14558 | 2130 | 836 | 1456 | 18980 |
| 36 | 10437 | 1541 | 702 | 1377 | 14057 |
| 37 | 8782 | 1268 | 477 | 1293 | 11820 |
| 38 | 10025 | 1416 | 579 | 1326 | 13346 |
| 39 | 7200 | 979 | 416 | 1001 | 9596 |
| 40 | 10886 | 1441 | 649 | 1019 | 13995 |
| 41 | 5634 | 822 | 320 | 659 | 7435 |
| 42 | 8369 | 1199 | 535 | 826 | 10929 |
| 43 | 7900 | 1079 | 533 | 828 | 10340 |
| 44 | 12274 | 1851 | 796 | 1149 | 16070 |
| 45 | 5509 | 954 | 289 | 260 | 7012 |
| 46 | 737 | 105 | 45 | 80 | 967 |
| 47 | 541 | 74 | 34 | 63 | 712 |
| 48 | 532 | 73 | 31 | 63 | 699 |
| 49 | 354 | 60 | 17 | 38 | 469 |
| 50 & over. | 1942 | 203 | 68 | 153 | 2366 |

The relative excess of the numbers at certain particular ages, and the corresponding defect at others, strikes the attention at the first glance. To the former class belong the ages, 21 years, most years divisible by 5 (excepting 20 and 45), and those divisible by 2; to the latter class belong most of those years of age whose last digit is 1 or 9. By determining the general law of distribution, we may obtain the measure of this excess, and thus throw light upon the origin of these discordances.

The following facts are also manifest, or readily deducible: —

Of the whole number, 1 012 273, about 1 per centum (.0102), were below, and a little more than one half as many (.0052) were above, the limits of military age, interpreted as between the ages 18 and 46.

Of the number 996 647, within these limits, —

| | |
|---|---|
| The average age at last birthday is   .   .   .   . | 25.3250 |
| The average age at time of enlistment is   .   .   . | 25.8083 |
| The age above and below which the numbers are equal is | 23.477 |
| There were of the age 18 years   .   .   .   . | 13.27 per cent. |
| under 21 years   .   .   .   . | 29.52 " |
| under 25 years   .   .   .   . | 58.34 " |
| under 30 years   .   .   .   . | 76.57 " |

The very close accordance of the proportional numbers for the total face of about a million of men from all the loyal States, with those deduced* by Mr. ELLIOTT for less than 51 000 men from the single State of Massachusetts, is very striking. Tables for the individual States and groups of States, herewith presented, unite in corroborating the inference that this distribution is due to no special local influences, but to a general and overruling law, which varies but slightly through widely distant regions of our country, and seems scarcely affected by any influences dependent upon immigration from abroad.

This law, which was found by Mr. ELLIOTT to hold good also for the Massachusetts troops, shows the number of volunteers (enlisted men, not including officers) at each successive year of age to form a series of which the first differences are in geometrical progression.

· When the ratio of this geometrical progression is unity, the

---

* " On the Military Statistics of the United States of America," Proceedings of the International Statistical Congress, V Session, 1863, p. 32.

progression becomes arithmetical; when, as in the present case, it is less than unity, we have a decreasing rate of change.

Let this ratio be denoted by $h$, and the number of men at any given year of age be

$$x_n = b + c \, (1 - h) \, h^n \tag{1}$$

so that the total number at and over that age will be

$$s_n = a - b n + c \, h^n \tag{2}$$

in which $n$ denotes the excess of the age above 18 years, at which epoch

$$s_0 = a + c.$$

The constants $a$, $b$, $c$, $h$ are to be determined, and we have

$$\Delta x_0 = c \, (1 - h)^2, \qquad \Delta x_n = c \, h^n \, (1 - h)^2, \qquad \Delta_m x_{mn} = c \, h^{mn} \, (1 - h^m)^2$$

whence

$$h^n = \frac{\Delta_m x_{mn}}{\Delta_m x_{(m+1)\,n}} \tag{3}$$

which enables us to determine $h$ from the most convenient equidistant portions of the series.

The variation of the fundamental equation (2) gives for any change in the values of the constants

$$\partial s_n = \partial a - n \, \partial b + h^n \, \partial c + n \, c \, h^{n-1} \, \partial h, \tag{4}$$

by means of which, after an approximate value of $h$ has been deduced from (3), and corresponding values of $a$, $b$, $c$ derived from the numerical data for any four years, the corrected values of all four constants may be derived by the method of least squares.

The total number up to any given age, or the definite sum from $x_0$ to $x_n$, is evidently

$$s_0 - s_n = b n + c \, (1 - h^n) = \Sigma_0^n x \tag{5}$$

so that

$$- n + \frac{c}{b} h^n = \frac{1}{b} \, (c - \Sigma_0^n x)$$

or by (2)

$$= \frac{1}{b} \, (s_n - a). \tag{6}$$

Since the numerical values deduced from the tables belong not to the age $n$ years, but to that age which corresponds to the average for all the individuals between $n$ and $n+1$ years, the constants deduced hold good also for the series of these mean ages; the successive annual arguments being really at intervals differing slightly from one year.

The age $t$ corresponding to this average may be deduced for any year with sufficient accuracy for all practical purposes, by putting $n = t$ in the first member of equation (6), and using in the last member the value of $s_{n+1}$ instead of $s_n$, which gives

$$- t + \frac{c}{b} h^t = \frac{1}{b} (s_{n+1} - a). \tag{7}$$

Similarly we may find the age corresponding to the average for any period of years. For this purpose we replace $s_{n+1}$ in the last member of the equation (7) by

$$\tfrac{1}{2} (s_n + s_{n'}) = a - \tfrac{1}{2} b (n + n') + \tfrac{1}{2} c (h^n + h^{n'})$$

and the corresponding value of $t$ is the age equivalent to the average of the period included between $n$ and $n'$.

Proceeding as above described, and, after the first approximate determination of $h$, $a$, $b$, $c$, from four conveniently situated and equidistant observed values of $s_n$, obtaining improved values for all four constants by the method of least squares, the formulas derived from the grand total of all the enlisted men of military age as presented in Table I. are these, which express the relative numbers for every ten thousand : —

$$x_n = \qquad\quad + 77.04 \quad + 1156.0 \cdot 0.85362^n$$
$$s_n = 2102.8 - 77.04\,n + 7897.2 \cdot 0.85362^n.$$

With these values the fourth and seventh columns of Table II. are computed, the third and sixth columns showing the "observed," or recorded numbers, reduced to the same scale; and the fifth and eighth columns exhibiting the discordances between the calculated and observed values.

These discordances, although in one sense regular, inasmuch as the larger ones are apparently not the result of so-called accident, or, in other words, of the use of numbers insufficient to eliminate discordances of no palpable significance, are in another sense markedly devoid of regularity, inasmuch as the positive and negative signs alternate freely, and no decided indication seems to exist of a systematic deviation of the general formula.

# TABLE II.

*Grand Total of Enlisted Men.*

| Age at last birthday. | Number. | Proportion at and over given age. | | Difference. (C. — O.) | Proportion at given age. | | Difference. (C. — O.) |
|---|---|---|---|---|---|---|---|
| | | Observed. | Calculated. | | Observed. | Calculated. | |
| 13 | 127 | | | | | | |
| 14 | 330 | | | | | | |
| 15 | 773 | | | | | | |
| 16 | 2758 | | | | | | |
| 17 | 6425 | | | | | | |
| 18 | 133475 | 10000 | 10000 | 0 | 1339 | 1233 | −106 |
| 19 | 90215 | ·8661 | 8767 | +106 | 905 | 1064 | +159 |
| 20 | 71058 | 7756 | 7703 | − 53 | 713 | 919 | +206 |
| 21 | 97136 | 7043 | 6784 | −259 | 975 | 796 | −179 |
| 22 | 73391 | 6068 | 5988 | − 80 | 736 | 691 | − 45 |
| 23 | 62717 | 5332 | 5297 | − 35 | 629 | 601 | − 28 |
| 24 | 52095 | 4703 | 4696 | − 7 | 523 | 524 | + 1 |
| 25 | 46626 | 4180 | 4172 | − 8 | 468 | 460 | − 8 |
| 26 | 40243 | 3712 | 3712 | 0 | 404 | 403 | − 1 |
| 27 | 34286 | 3308 | 3309 | + 1 | 344 | 355 | + 11 |
| 28 | 35312 | 2964 | 2954 | − 10 | 354 | 315 | − 39 |
| 29 | 24513 | 2610 | 2641 | + 31 | 246 | 280 | + 34 |
| 30 | 28360 | 2364 | 2361 | − 3 | 285 | 250 | − 35 |
| 31 | 17954 | 2079 | 2111 | + 32 | 181 | 225 | + 44 |
| 32 | 21967 | 1898 | 1886 | − 12 | 221 | 203 | − 18 |
| 33 | 17979 | 1677 | 1683 | + 6 | 181 | 185 | + 4 |
| 34 | 15740 | 1496 | 1498 | + 2 | 158 | 169 | + 11 |
| 35 | 18980 | 1338 | 1329 | − 9 | 191 | 156 | − 35 |
| 36 | 14057 | 1147 | 1173 | + 26 | 141 | 144 | + 3 |
| 37 | 11820 | 1006 | 1029 | + 23 | 118 | 134 | + 16 |
| 38 | 13346 | 888 | 895 | + 7 | 133 | 126 | − 7 |
| 39 | 9596 | 755 | 769 | + 14 | 96 | 118 | + 22 |
| 40 | 13995 | 659 | 651 | − 8 | 141 | 112 | − 29 |
| 41 | 7435 | 518 | 539 | + 21 | 74 | 107 | + 33 |
| 42 | 10929 | 444 | 432 | − 12 | 109 | 103 | − 6 |
| 43 | 10340 | 335 | 329 | − 6 | 104 | 99 | − 5 |
| 44 | 16070 | 231 | 230 | − 1 | 161 | 96 | − 65 |
| 45 | 7012 | 70 | 134 | + 64 | 70 | 93 | + 23 |
| 46 | 967 | | | | | | |
| 47 | 712 | | | | | | |
| 48 | 699 | | | | | | |
| 49 | 469 | | | | | | |
| 50 & over. | 2366 | | | | | | |

The trustworthiness of the equations from which the "calculated" numbers in this table are derived will be readily estimated upon inspection of the two columns which exhibit the difference between the calculated and observed numbers at the different years of age; and the substitution of the numerical values of the constants in equations (6) and (7) enables us to determine without difficulty the actual average age which corresponds to any given "age last birthday."

Making these numerical substitutions, the equations assume the form

$$-n + 102.507 \, (0.85362)^n = -27.2949 + 0.01298027 \, s_n \qquad (8)$$

$$t - 102.507 \, (0.85362)^t = -27.2949 + 0.01298027 \, s_{n+1} \qquad (9)$$

and yield at once the true ages corresponding to the average of the ages "at last birthday," which will be found as follows: —

| Age last birthday. | Corresponding average age. |
|---|---|
| 18 | 18.4814 |
| 23 | 23.4826 |
| 28 | 28.4843 |
| 33 | 33.4885 |
| 38 | 38.4924 |
| 43 | 43.4956 |
| 45 | 45.4968 |

Intermediate values may be found by interpolation with all needful accuracy.

Tables similar to Table II. prepared for each arm of the services independently, and for nine States or groups of States, and numbered as Tables III. to XIV. inclusive, are appended.

Such tables were originally constructed for a much larger number of groups; but these twelve will abundantly suffice to make manifest all the marked phenomena which the more detailed series has brought to light.

# TABLE III.

## United States Volunteer Infantry.

| Age at last birthday. | Number at each year of age. | Proportion at and over specified age. | | Difference. (C. — O.) | Proportion at each year of age. | | Difference. (C. — O.) |
|---|---|---|---|---|---|---|---|
| | | Observed. | Calculated. | | Observed. | Calculated. | |
| 13 | 113 | | | | | | |
| 14 | 288 | | | | | | |
| 15 | 636 | | | | | | |
| 16 | 2053 | | | | | | |
| 17 | 4653 | | | | | | |
| 18 | 103420 | 10000 | 10000 | 0 | 1337 | 1252 | − 85 |
| 19 | 71226 | 8663 | 8748 | + 85 | 921 | 1078 | +157 |
| 20 | 56238 | 7742 | 7670 | − 72 | 727 | 921 | +194 |
| 21 | 75978 | 7015 | 6749 | −266 | 983 | 802 | −181 |
| 22 | 57485 | 6032 | 5947 | − 85 | 743 | 694 | − 49 |
| 23 | 48954 | 5289 | 5253 | − 36 | 633 | 602 | − 31 |
| 24 | 40852 | 4656 | 4651 | − 5 | 528 | 524 | − 4 |
| 25 | 36383 | 4128 | 4127 | − 1 | 470 | 458 | − 12 |
| 26 | 31292 | 3658 | 3669 | + 11 | 405 | 401 | − 4 |
| 27 | 26369 | 3253 | 3268 | + 15 | 341 | 353 | + 12 |
| 28 | 27196 | 2912 | 2915 | + 3 | 352 | 312 | − 40 |
| 29 . | 18833 | 2560 | 2603 | .+ 43 | 244 | 276 | + 32 |
| 30 | 21937 | 2316 | 2327 | + 11 | 284 | 247 | − 37 |
| 31 | 12814 | 2032 | 2080 | + 48 | 166 | 221 | + 55 |
| 32 | 17038 | 1866 | 1859 | − 7 | 220 | 200 | − 20 |
| 33 | 13678 | 1646 | 1659 | + 13 | 177 | 181 | + 4 |
| 34 | 12004 | 1469 | 1478 | + 9 | 155 | 166 | + 11 |
| 35 | 14558 | 1314 | 1312 | − 2 | 188 | 152 | − 36 |
| 36 | 10437 | 1126 | 1160 | + 34 | 135 | 141 | + 6 |
| 37 | 8782 | 991 | 1019 | + 28 | 114 | 131 | + 17 |
| 38 | 10025 | 877 | 888 | + 11 | 130 | 123 | − 7 |
| 39 | 7200 | 747 | 765 | + 18 | 93 | 116 | + 23 |
| 40 | 10886 | 654 | 649 | − 5 | 141 | 110 | − 31 |
| 41 | 5634 | 513 | 539 | + 26 | 73 | 105 | + 32 |
| 42 | 8369 | 440 | 434 | − 6 | 108 | 101 | − 7 |
| 43 | 7900 | 332 | 333 | + 1 | 102 | 97 | − 5 |
| 44 | 12274 | 230 | 236 | + 6 | 159 | 94 | − 65 |
| 45 | 5509 | 71 | 142 | + 71 | 71 | 91 | + 20 |
| 46 | 737 | | | | | | |
| 47 | 541 | | | | | | |
| 48 | 532 | | | | | | |
| 49 | 354 | | | | | | |
| 50 | 1942 | | | | | | |

# TABLE IV.

## *United States Volunteer Cavalry.*

| Age at last birthday. | Number. at each year of age. | Proportion at and over specified age. | | Difference. (C. — O.) | Proportion at each year of age. | | Difference. (C. — O.) |
|---|---|---|---|---|---|---|---|
| | | Observed. | Calculated. | | Observed. | Calculated. | |
| 13 | 5 | | | | | | |
| 14 | 15 | | | | | | |
| 15 | 49 | | | | | | |
| 16 | 232 | | | | | | |
| 17 | 638 | | | | | | |
| 18 | 15013 | 10000 | 10000 | 0 | 1295 | 1240 | — 55 |
| 19 | 9767 | 8705 | 8760 | + 55 | 842 | 1074 | +232 |
| 20 | 7864 | 7863 | 7686 | —177 | 682 | 931 | +249 |
| 21 | 12081 | 7181 | 6755 | —426 | 1042 | 808 | —234 |
| 22 | 9096 | 6139 | 5947 | —192 | 784 | 703 | — 81 |
| 23 | 7806 | 5355 | 5244 | —111 | 673 | 612 | — 61 |
| 24 | 6361 | 4682 | 4632 | — 50 | 549 | 534 | — 15 |
| 25 | 5724 | 4133 | 4098 | — 35 | 494 | 467 | — 27 |
| 26 | 4831 | 3639 | 3631 | — 8 | 417 | 410 | — 7 |
| 27 | 4192 | 3222 | 3221 | — 1 | 360 | 360 | 0 |
| 28 | 4318 | 2862 | 2861 | — 1 | 372 | 318 | — 54 |
| 29 | 2845 | 2490 | 2543 | + 53 | 245 | 281 | +, 36 |
| 30 | 3251 | 2245 | 2262 | + 17 | 280 | 250 | — 30 |
| 31 | 2043 | 1965 | 2012 | + 47 | 176 | 223 | + 47 |
| 32 | 2450 | 1789 | 1789 | 0 | 211 | 200 | — 11 |
| 33 | 1950 | 1578 | 1589 | + 11 | 168 | 180 | + 12 |
| 34 | 1679 | 1410 | 1410 | 0 | 145 | 163 | + 18 |
| 35 | 2130 | 1265 | 1247 | — 18 | 184 | 148 | — 36 |
| 36 | 1541 | 1081 | 1098 | + 17 | 133 | 135 | + 2 |
| 37 | 1268 | 948 | 963 | + 15 | 109 | 124 | + 15 |
| 38 | 1416 | 839 | 839 | 0 | 122 | 115 | — 7 |
| 39 | 979 | 717 | 724 | + 7 | 84 | 107 | + 23 |
| 40 | 1441 | 633 | 618 | — 15 | 124 | 100 | — 24 |
| 41 | 822 | 509 | 518 | + 8 | 71 | 94 | + 23 |
| 42 | 1199 | 438 | 426 | — 12 | 103 | 89 | — 14 |
| 43 | 1079 | 335 | 337 | + 2 | 93 | 85 | — 8 |
| 44 | 1851 | 242 | 252 | + 10 | 160 | 81 | — 79 |
| 45 | 954 | 82 | 170 | + 88 | 82 | 78 | — 4 |
| 46 | 105 | | | | | | |
| 47 | 74 | | | | | | |
| 48 | 73 | | | | | | |
| 49 | 60 | | | | | | |
| 50 | 203 | | | | | | |

# TABLE V.

## *United States Volunteer Artillery.*

| Age at last birthday. | Number at each year of age. | Proportion at and over specified age. | | Difference. (C. — O.) | Proportion at each year of age. | | Difference. (C. — O.) |
|---|---|---|---|---|---|---|---|
| | | Observed. | Calculated. | | Observed. | Calculated. | |
| 14 | 2 | | | | | | |
| 15 | 21 | | | | | | |
| 16 | 61 | | | | | | |
| 17 | 226 | | | | | | |
| 18 | 5400 | 10000 | 10000 | 0 | 1275 | 1179 | − 96 |
| 19 | 3439 | 8725 | 8821 | + 96 | 812 | 1024 | +212 |
| 20 | 2627 | 7913 | 7797 | −116 | 620 | 891 | +271 |
| 21 | 4416 | 7293 | 6906 | −387 | 1042 | 776 | −266 |
| 22 | 3107 | 6251 | 6130 | −121 | • 734 | 678 | − 56 |
| 23 | 2759 | 5517 | 5452 | − 65 | 651 | 593 | − 58 |
| 24 | 2163 | 4866 | 4859 | − 7 | 511 | 521 | + 10 |
| 25 | 2012 | 4355 | 4338 | − 17 | 475 | 459 | − 16 |
| 26 | 1768 | 3880 | 3879 | − 1 | 417 | 405 | − 12 |
| 27 | 1505 | 3463 | 3474 | + 11 | 355 | 359 | + 4 |
| 28 | 1525 | 3108 | 3115 | + 7 | 360 | 320 | − 40 |
| 29 | 1087 | 2748 | 2795 | + 47 | 257 | 286 | + 29 |
| 30 | 1213 | 2491 | 2509 | + 18 | 286 | 257 | − 29 |
| 31 | 796 | 2205 | 2252 | + 47 | 188 | 232 | + 44 |
| 32 | 931 | 2017 | 2020 | + 3 | 220 | 211 | − 9 |
| 33 | 753 | 1797 | 1809 | + 12 | 178 | 193 | + 15 |
| 34 | 724 | 1619 | 1616 | − 3 | 171 | 177 | + 6 |
| 35 | 836 | 1448 | 1439 | − 9 | 197 | 163 | − 34 |
| 36 | 702 | 1251 | 1276 | + 25 | 166 | 151 | − 15 |
| 37 | 477 | 1085 | 1125 | + 40 | 113 | 142 | + 29 |
| 38 | 579 | 972 | 983 | + 11 | 137 | 133 | − 4 |
| 39 | 416 | 835 | 850 | + 15 | 98 | 126 | + 28 |
| 40 | 649 | 737 | 724 | − 13 | 153 | 119 | − 34 |
| 41 | 320 | 584 | 605 | + 21 | 76 | 114 | + 38 |
| 42 | 535 | 508 | 491 | − 17 | 126 | 109 | − 17 |
| 43 | 533 | 382 | 382 | 0 | 126 | 105 | − 21 |
| 44 | 796 | 256 | 277 | + 21 | 188 | 102 | − 86 |
| 45 | 289 | 68 | 175 | +107 | 68 | 100 | + 32 |
| 46 | 45 | | | | | | |
| 47 | 34 | | | | | | |
| 48 | 31 | | | | | | |
| 49 | 17 | | | | | | |
| 50 | 68 | | | | | | |

## TABLE VI.

*Ages of Maine, New Hampshire, Vermont, and Connecticut Vol's.*

| Age at last birthday. | Number. at each year of age. | Proportion at and over specified age. | | Difference. (C. — O.) | Proportion at each year of age. | | Difference. (C. — O.) |
|---|---|---|---|---|---|---|---|
| | | Observed. | Calculated. | | Observed. | Calculated. | |
| 13 | 3 | | | | | | |
| 14 | 10 | | | | | | |
| 15 | 27 | | | | | | |
| 16 | 95 | | | | | | |
| 17 | 223 | | | | | | |
| 18 | 11694 | 10000 | 10001 | + 1 | 1522 | 1245 | −277 |
| 19 | 6541 | 8478 | 8756 | +278 | 852 | 1071 | +219 |
| 20 | 5311 | 7626 | 7685 | + 59 | 691 | 923 | +232 |
| 21 | 7477 | 6935 | 6762 | −173 | 976 | 800 | −176 |
| 22 | 5356 | 5959 | 5962 | + 3 | 699 | 685 | − 14 |
| 23 | 4614 | 5260 | 5277 | + 17 | 604 | 598 | − 6 |
| 24 | 3824 | 4656 | 4679 | + 23 | 500 | 519 | + 19 |
| 25 | 3357 | 4156 | 4160 | + 4 | 440 | 453 | + 13 |
| 26 | 2988 | 3716 | 3707 | − 9 | 390 | 397 | + 7 |
| 27 | 2590 | 3326 | 3310 | − 16 | 338 | 350 | + 12 |
| 28 | 2762 | 2988 | 2960 | − 28 | 361 | 307 | − 54 |
| 29 | 1881 | 2627 | 2653 | + 26 | 245 | 273 | + 28 |
| 30 | 1983 | 2382 | 2380 | − 2 | 259 | 243 | − 16 |
| 31 | 1362 | 2123 | 2137 | + 14 | 177 | 218 | + 41 |
| 32 | 1609 | 1946 | 1919 | − 27 | 210 | 196 | − 14 |
| 33 | 1427 | 1736 | 1723 | − 13 | 185 | 178 | − 7 |
| 34 | 1141 | 1551 | 1545 | − 6 | 149 | 163 | + 14 |
| 35 | 1355 | 1402 | 1382 | − 20 | 176 | 149 | − 27 |
| 36 | 1046 | 1226 | 1233 | + 7 | 136 | 138 | + 2 |
| 37 | 989 | 1090 | 1095 | + 5 | 127 | 128 | + 1 |
| 38 | 1005 | 963 | 967 | + 4 | 131 | 118 | − 13 |
| 39 | 817 | 832 | 849 | + 17 | 107 | 115 | + 8 |
| 40 | 969 | 725 | 734 | + 9 | 127 | 108 | − 19 |
| 41 | 604 | 598 | 626 | + 28 | 77 | 102 | + 25 |
| 42 | 882 | 521 | 524 | + 3 | 115 | 97 | − 18 |
| 43 | 870 | 406 | 427 | + 21 | 113 | 95 | − 18 |
| 44 | 1789 | 293 | 332 | + 39 | 233 | 90 | −143 |
| 45 | 459 | 60 | 242 | +182 | 60 | 88 | + 28 |
| 46 | 50 | | | | | | |
| 47 | 38 | | | | | | |
| 48 | 34 | | | | | | |
| 49 | 23 | | | | | | |
| 50 & over. | 60 | | | | | | |

# TABLE VII.

## Ages of Massachusetts Volunteers.

| Age at last birthday. | Number at each year of age. | Proportion at and over specified age. | | Difference. (C. — O.) | Proportion at each year of age. | | Difference. (C. — O.) |
|---|---|---|---|---|---|---|---|
| | | Observed. | Calculated. | | Observed. | Calculated. | |
| 12 | 4 | · | | | | | |
| 13 | 4 | | | | | | |
| 14 | 26 | | | | | | |
| 15 | 44 | | | | | | |
| 16 | 101 | | | | | | |
| 17 | 289 | | | | | | |
| 18 | 6894 | 10000 | 10000 | 0 | 1269 | 1145 | −124 |
| 19 | 4582 | 8731 | 8855 | +124 | 846 | 1002 | +156 |
| 20 | 3604 | 7885 | 7853 | − 32 | 666 | 877 | +211 |
| 21 | 5429 | 7219 | 6976 | −243 | 1003 | 771 | −232 |
| 22 | 3860 | 6216 | 6205 | − 11 | 713 | 678 | − 35 |
| 23 | 3203 | 5513 | 5527 | + 14 | 592 | 597 | + 5 |
| 24 | 2871 | 4921 | 4930 | + 9 | 530 | 528 | − 2 |
| 25 | 2474 | 4391 | 4402 | + 11 | 457 | 467 | + 10 |
| 26 | 2232 | 3934 | 3935 | + 1 | 412 | 415 | + 3 |
| 27 | 1962 | 3522 | 3520 | − 2 | 362 | 370 | + 8 |
| 28 | 2041 | 3160 | 3150 | − 10 | 377 | 330 | − 47 |
| 29 | 1411 | 2783 | 2820 | + 37 | 260 | 296 | + 36 |
| 30 | 1564 | 2523 | 2524 | + 1 | 288 | 267 | − 21 |
| 31 | 988 | 2235 | 2257 | + 22 | 183 | 242 | + 59 |
| 32 | 1233 | 2042 | 2015 | − 27 | 228 | 219 | − 9 |
| 33 | 1041 | 1814 | 1796 | − 18 | 193 | 200 | + 7 |
| 34 | 980 | 1621 | 1596 | − 25 | 181 | 184 | + 3 |
| 35 | 1213 | 1440 | 1412 | − 28 | 224 | 169 | − 55 |
| 36 | 761 | 1216 | 1243 | + 27 | 141 | 157 | + 16 |
| 37 | 699 | 1075 | 1086 | + 11 | 129 | 146 | + 17 |
| 38 | 828 | 946 | 940 | − 6 | 153 | 137 | − 16 |
| 39 | 600 | 793 | 803 | + 10 | 111 | 129 | + 18 |
| 40 | 838 | 682 | 674 | − 8 | 155 | 122 | − 33 |
| 41 | 440 | 527 | 552 | + 25 | 81 | 116 | + 35 |
| 42 | 658 | 446 | 436 | − 10 | 122 | 110 | − 12 |
| 43 | 596 | 324 | 326 | + 2 | 110 | 106 | − 4 |
| 44 | 859 | 214 | 220 | + 6 | 159 | 102 | − 57 |
| 45 | 296 | 55 | 118 | + 63 | 55 | 98 | + 43 |
| 46 | 28 | | | | | | |
| 47 | 14 | | | | | | |
| 48 | 16 | | | | | | |
| 49 | 9 | | | | | | |
| 50 & over. | 33 | | | | | | |

## TABLE VIII.

### *Ages of New York Volunteers.*

| Age at last birthday. | Number. at each year of age. | Proportion at and over specified age. | | Difference. (C. — O.) | Proportion at each year of age. | | Difference. (C. — O.) |
|---|---|---|---|---|---|---|---|
| | | Observed. | Calculated. | | Observed. | Calculated. | |
| 13 | 17 | | | | | | |
| 14 | 63 | | | | | | |
| 15 | 153 | | | | | | |
| 16 | 448 | | | | | | |
| 17 | 699 | | | | | | |
| 18 | 19737 | 10000 | 10000 | 0 | 1087 | 1173 | + 86 |
| 19 | 16233 | 8913 | 8827 | − 86 | 894 | 1019 | +125 |
| 20 | 11286 | 8019 | 7808 | −211 | 621 | 887 | +266 |
| 21 | 20227 | 7398 | 6922 | −476 | 1114 | 773 | −341 |
| 22 | 13689 | 6284 | 6149 | −135 | 754 | 675 | − 79 |
| 23 | 11516 | 5530 | 5774 | +244 | 634 | 592 | − 42 |
| 24 | 9488 | 4896 | 4882 | − 14 | 523 | 520 | − 3 |
| 25 | 8648 | 4373 | 4363 | − 10 | 476 | 459 | − 17 |
| 26 | 7285 | 3897 | 3904 | + 7 | 401 | 406 | + 5 |
| 27 | 6223 | 3496 | 3498 | + 2 | 343 | 360 | + 17 |
| 28 | 6652 | 3153 | 3138 | − 15 | 366 | 322 | − 44 |
| 29 | 4552 | 2787 | 2816 | + 29 | 251 | 289 | + 38 |
| 30 | 5474 | 2536 | 2527 | − 9 | 301 | 260 | − 41 |
| 31 | 3287 | 2235 | 2267 | + 32 | 181 | 236 | + 55 |
| 32. | 4533 | 2054 | 2031 | − 23 | 249 | 215 | − 34 |
| 33 | 3330 | 1805 | 1816 | + 11 | 184 | 197 | + 13 |
| 34 | 3135 | 1621 | 1619 | − 2 | 173 | 182 | + 9 |
| 35 | 3885 | 1448 | 1437 | − 11 | 114 | 168 | + 54 |
| 36 | 2872 | 1234 | 1269 | + 35 | 158 | 157 | − 1 |
| 37 | 2201 | 1076 | 1112 | + 36 | 121 | 146 | + 25 |
| 38 | 2709 | 955 | 966 | + 11 | 149 | 139 | − 10 |
| 39 | 1858 | 806 | 827 | + 21 | 103 | 132 | + 29 |
| 40 | 3157 | 703 | 695 | − 8 | 173 | 126 | − 47 |
| 41 | 1268 | 530 | 569 | + 39 | 70 | 121 | + 51 |
| 42 | 2302 | 460 | 448 | − 12 | 127 | 116 | − 11 |
| 43 | 2068 | 333 | 332 | − 1 | 114 | 112 | − 2 |
| 44 | 3148 | 219 | 220 | + 1 | 173 | 109 | − 64 |
| 45 | 831 | 46 | 111 | + 65 | 46 | 106 | + 60 |
| 46 | 87 | | | | | | |
| 47 | 41 | | | | | | |
| 48 | 53 | | | | | | |
| 49 | 23 | | | | | | |
| 50 & over. | 103 | | | | | | |

# TABLE IX.

### Ages of Pennsylvania Volunteers (including Reserves).

| Age at last birthday. | Number at each year of age. | Proportion at and over specified age. | | Difference. (C. — O.) | Proportion at each year of age. | | Difference. (C. — O.) |
|---|---|---|---|---|---|---|---|
| | | Observed. | Calculated. | | Observed. | Calculated. | |
| 13 | 23 | | | | | | |
| 14 | 51 | | | | | | |
| 15 | 85 | | | | | | |
| 16 | 241 | | | | | | |
| 17 | 486 | | | | | | |
| 18 | 13052 | 10000 | 10000 | 0 | 1137 | 1339 | +202 |
| 19 | 11410 | 8863 | 8661 | −202 | 994 | 1131 | +137 |
| 20 | 8234 | 7869 | 7530 | −339 | 717 | 959 | +242 |
| 21 | 13336 | 7152 | 6571 | −581 | 1161 | 814 | −347 |
| 22 | 9376 | 5991 | 5757 | −234 | 816 | 694 | −122 |
| 23 | 7696 | 5175 | 5063 | −112 | 670 | 595 | − 75 |
| 24 | 6061 | 4505 | 4468 | − 37 | 528 | 510 | − 18 |
| 25 | 5375 | 3977 | 3958 | − 19 | 468 | 441 | − 27 |
| 26 | 4420 | 3509 | 3517 | + 8 | 385 | 382 | − 3 |
| 27 | 3576 | 3124 | 3135 | + 11 | 311 | 334 | + 23 |
| 28 | 3817 | 2813 | 2801 | − 12 | 332 | 293 | − 39 |
| 29 | 2644 | 2481 | 2508 | + 27 | 230 | 260 | + 30 |
| 30 | 2926 | 2251 | 2248 | − 3 | 255 | 232 | − 23 |
| 31 | 2029 | 1996 | 2016 | + 20 | 177 | 208 | + 31 |
| 32 | 2375 | 1819 | 1808 | − 11 | 207 | 188 | − 19 |
| 33 | 1903 | 1612 | 1620 | + 8 | 166 | 173 | + 7 |
| 34 | 1657 | 1446 | 1447 | + 1 | 144 | 159 | + 14 |
| 35 | 2089 | 1302 | 1289 | − 13 | 182 | 147 | − 35 |
| 36 | 1490 | 1120 | 1142 | + 22 | 130 | 138 | + 8 |
| 37 | 1290 | 990 | 1004 | + 14 | 112 | 130 | + 18 |
| 38 | 1434 | 878 | 874 | − 4 | 125 | 124 | − 1 |
| 39 | 1141 | 753 | 750 | − 3 | 99 | 118 | + 19 |
| 40 | 1692 | 654 | 632 | − 22 | 147 | 113 | − 34 |
| 41 | 918 | 507 | 519 | + 12 | 80 | 109 | + 29 |
| 42 | 1431 | 427 | 410 | + 17 | 124 | 106 | − 18 |
| 43 | 1318 | 303 | 307 | + 4 | 115 | 103 | − 12 |
| 44 | 1674 | 188 | 206 | + 18 | 146 | 101 | − 45 |
| 45 | 480 | 42 | 105 | + 63 | 42 | 99 | + 57 |
| 46 | 73 | | | | | | |
| 47 | 46 | | | | | | |
| 48 | 49 | | | | | | |
| 49 | 36 | | | | | | |
| 50 & over. | 109 | | | | | | |

# TABLE X.

## *Ages of Ohio Volunteers.*

| Age at last birthday. | Number at each year of age. | Proportion at and over specified age. | | Difference. (C. — O.) | Proportion at each year of age. | | Difference. (C. — O.) |
|---|---|---|---|---|---|---|---|
| | | Observed. | Calculated. | | Observed. | Calculated. | |
| 13 | 21 | | | | | | |
| 14 | 44 | | | | | | |
| 15 | 103 | | | | | | |
| 16 | 470 | | | | | | |
| 17 | 1476 | | | | | | |
| 18 | 23495 | 10000 | 10000 | 0 | 1567 | 1359 | —208 |
| 19 | 14986 | 8433 | 8641 | +208 | 999 | 1143 | +144 |
| 20 | 12358 | 7434 | 7498 | + 64 | 825 | 963 | +138 |
| 21 | 12819 | 6609 | 6535 | — 74 | 855 | 815 | — 40 |
| 22 | 10499 | 5754 | 5720 | — 34 | 700 | 692 | — 8 |
| 23 | 9297 | 5054 | 5028 | — 26 | 620 | 590 | — 30 |
| 24 | 7327 | 4434 | 4438 | — 6 | 489 | 505 | + 16 |
| 25 | 6502 | 3945 | 3933 | — 12 | 430 | 435 | + 5 |
| 26 | 5678 | 3515 | 3498 | — 17 | 382 | 377 | — 5 |
| 27 | 4739 | 3133 | 3121 | — 12 | 316 | 329 | + 13 |
| 28 | 4997 | 2817 | 2792 | — 25 | 333 | 289 | — 44 |
| 29 | 3570 | 2484 | 2503 | + 19 | 238 | 256 | + 18 |
| 30 | 3960 | 2246 | 2247 | + 1 | 264 | 228 | — 36 |
| 31 | 2596 | 1992 | 2019 | + 37 | 174 | 206 | + 32 |
| 32 | 3029 | 1808 | 1813 | + 5 | 201 | 187 | — 14 |
| 33 | 2669 | 1607 | 1626 | + 19 | 178 | 171 | — 7 |
| 34 | 2302 | 1429 | 1455 | + 26 | 154 | 159 | + 5 |
| 35 | 2659 | 1275 | 1296 | + 21 | 178 | 148 | — 30 |
| 36 | 2216 | •1097 | 1148 | + 51 | 147 | 139 | — 8 |
| 37 | 1830 | 950 | 1009 | + 59 | 123 | 132 | + 9 |
| 38 | 1959 | 827 | 877 | + 50. | 130 | 125 | — 5 |
| 39 | 1424 | 697 | 752 | + 55 | 95 | 120 | + 25 |
| 40 | 1880 | 602 | 632 | + 30 | 126 | 116 | — 10 |
| 41 | 1097 | 476 | 516 | + 40 | 73 | 113 | + 40 |
| 42 | 1513 | 403 | 403 | 0 | 101 | 110 | + 9 |
| 43 | 1337 | 302 | 293 | — 9 | 89 | 108 | + 19 |
| 44 | 2070 | 213 | 185 | — 28 | 138 | 106 | — 32 |
| 45 | 1128 | 75 | 79 | + 4 | 75 | 104 | + 29 |
| 46 | 202 | | | | | | |
| 47 | 161 | | | | | | |
| 48 | 145 | | | | | | |
| 49 | 104 | | | | | | |
| 50 & over. | 471 | | | | | | |

## TABLE XI.

### *Ages of Indiana Volunteers.*

| Age at last birthday. | Number at each year of age. | Proportion at and over specified age. | | Difference. (C. — O.) | Proportion at each year of age. | | Difference. (C. — O.) |
|---|---|---|---|---|---|---|---|
| | | Observed. | Calculated. | | Observed. | Calculated. | |
| 13 | 13 | | | | | | |
| 14 | 16 | | | | | | |
| 15 | 39 | | | | | | |
| 16 | 162 | | | | | | |
| 17 | 578 | | | | | | |
| 18 | 11178 | 10000 | 10000 | 0 | 1608 | 1446 | −162 |
| 19 | 7175 | 8392 | 8554 | +162 | 1032 | 1223 | +191 |
| 20 | 6478 | 7360 | 7331 | − 29 | 932 | 1035 | +103 |
| 21 | 6398 | 6428 | 6296 | −132 | 920 | 877 | − 43 |
| 22 | 5580 | 5508 | 5419 | − 89 | 802 | 744 | − 58 |
| 23 | 4562 | 4706 | 4675 | − 31 | 656 | 632 | − 24 |
| 24 | 3782 | 4050 | 4043 | − 7 | 544 | 538 | − 6 |
| 25 | 3216 | 3506 | 3505 | − 1 | 462 | 460 | − 2 |
| 26 | 2707 | 3044 | 3045 | + 1 | 390 | 394 | + 4 |
| 27 | 2269 | 2654 | 2651 | − 3 | 326 | 337 | + 11 |
| 28 | 2272 | 2328 | 2314 | − 14 | 327 | 290 | − 37 |
| 29 | 1513 | 2001 | 2024 | + 23 | 217 | 251 | + 34 |
| 30 | 1799 | 1784 | 1773 | − 11 | 259 | 218 | − 41 |
| 31 | 1013 | 1525 | 1555 | + 30 | 145 | 190 | + 45 |
| 32 | 1230 | 1380 | 1365 | − 15 | 177 | 166 | − 11 |
| 33 | 1046 | 1203 | 1200 | − 3 | 151 | 146 | − 5 |
| 34 | 871 | 1052 | 1053 | + 1 | 125 | 130 | + 5 |
| 35 | 962 | 927 | 923 | − 4 | 138 | 116 | − 22 |
| 36 | 666 | 789 | 806 | + 17 | 96 | 104 | + 8 |
| 37 | 589 | 693 | 702 | + 9 | 85 | 94 | + 9 |
| 38 | 656 | 608 | 608 | 0 | 94 | 86 | − 8 |
| 39 | 428 | 514 | 522 | + 8 | 62 | 79 | + 17 |
| 40 | 683 | 452 | 443 | − 9 | 98 | 73 | − 25 |
| 41 | 371 | 354 | 370 | + 16 | 53 | 68 | + 15 |
| 42 | 482 | 301 | 302 | + 1 | 69 | 64 | − 5 |
| 43 | 471 | 232 | 238 | + 6 | 68 | 60 | − 8 |
| 44 | 682 | 164 | 178 | + 14 | 98 | 57 | − 41 |
| 45 | 457 | 66 | 121 | + 55 | 66 | 55 | − 11 |
| 46 | 70 | | | | | | |
| 47 | 37 | | | | | | |
| 48 | 50 | | | | | | |
| 49 | 24 | | | | | | |
| 50 & over. | 146 | | | | | | |

# TABLE XII.

## *Ages of Michigan Volunteers.*

| Age at last birthday. | Number. at each year of age. | Proportion at and over specified age. | | Difference. (C. — O.) | Proportion at each year of age. | | Difference. (C. — O.) |
|---|---|---|---|---|---|---|---|
| | | Observed. | Calculated. | | Observed. | Calculated. | |
| 13 | 3 | | | | | | |
| 14 | 9 | | | | | | |
| 15 | 27 | | | | | | |
| 16 | 112 | | | | | | |
| 17 | 299 | | | | | | |
| 18 | 5862 | 10000 | 10000 | 0 | 1523 | 1279 | −244 |
| 19 | 3437 | 8477 | 8721 | +244 | 893 | 1098 | +205 |
| 20 | 2767 | 7584 | 7623 | + 39 | 719 | 943 | +224 |
| 21 | 3727 | 6865 | 6680 | −185 | 968 | 812 | −156 |
| 22 | 2802 | 5897 | 5868 | − 29 | 728 | 700 | − 28 |
| 23 | 2337 | 5169 | 5168 | − 1 | 607 | 605 | − 2 |
| 24 | 1963 | 4562 | 4563 | + 1 | 510 | 524 | + 14 |
| 25 | 1724 | 4052 | 4039 | − 13 | 448 | 455 | + 7 |
| 26 | 1568 | 3604 | 3584 | − 20 | 407 | 396 | − 11 |
| 27 | 1297 | 3197 | 3188 | − 9 | 337 | 346 | + 9 |
| 28 | 1335 | 2860 | 2842 | − 18 | 347 | 304 | − 43 |
| 29 | 923 | 2513 | 2538 | + 25 | 240 | 268 | + 28 |
| 30 | 989 | 2273 | 2270 | − 3 | 257 | 237 | − 20 |
| 31 | 695 | 2016 | 2033 | + 17 | 180 | 211 | + 31 |
| 32 | 843 | 1836 | 1822 | − 14 | 219 | 188 | − 31 |
| 33 | 614 | 1617 | 1634 | + 17 | 160 | 169 | + 9 |
| 34 | 527 | 1457 | 1465 | + 8 | 137 | 153 | + 16 |
| 35 | 668 | 1320 | 1312 | − 8 | 173 | 140 | − 33 |
| 36 | 481 | 1147 | 1172 | + 25 | 125 | 128 | + 3 |
| 37 | 411 | 1022 | 1044 | + 22 | 107 | 118 | + 11 |
| 38 | 458 | 915 | 926 | + 11 | 119 | 109 | − 10 |
| 39 | 313 | 796 | 817 | + 21 | 81 | 102 | + 21 |
| 40 | 466 | 715 | 715 | + 0 | 121 | 96 | − 25 |
| 41 | 256 | 594 | 619 | + 25 | 67 | 91 | + 24 |
| 42 | 403 | 527 | 528 | + 1 | 105 | 86 | − 19 |
| 43 | 400 | 422 | 442 | + 20 | 104 | 83 | − 21 |
| 44 | 825 | 318 | 359 | + 41 | 214 | 79 | −135 |
| 45 | 398 | 104 | 280 | +176 | 104 | 77 | − 27 |
| 46 | 44 | | | | | | |
| 47 | 23 | | | | | | |
| 48 | 26 | | | | | | |
| 49 | 14 | | | | | | |
| 50 & over. | 61 | | | | | | |

# TABLE XIII.

## *Ages of Illinois Volunteers.*

| Age at last birthday. | Number at each year of age. | Proportion at and over specified age. | | Difference. (C. — O.) | Proportion at each year of age. | | Difference. (C. — O.) |
|---|---|---|---|---|---|---|---|
| | | Observed. | Calculated. | | Observed. | Calculated. | |
| 13 | 5 | | | | | | |
| 14 | 23 | | | | | | |
| 15 | 65 | | | | | | |
| 16 | 250 | | | | | | |
| 17 | 539 | | | | | | |
| 18 | 10167 | 10000 | 10080 | + 80 | 1070 | 942 | −128 |
| 19 | 8348 | 8930 | 9138 | +208 | 879 | 1043 | +164 |
| 20 | 7076 | 8051 | 8095 | + 44 | 745 | 958 | +213 |
| 21 | 8709 | 7306 | 7137 | −169 | 916 | 858 | − 58 |
| 22 | 7441 | 6390 | 6279 | −111 | 783 | 766 | − 17 |
| 23 | 6872 | 5607 | 5513 | − 94 | 723 | 677 | − 46 |
| 24 | 6019 | 4884 | 4836 | − 48 | 634 | 600 | − 34 |
| 25 | 5315 | 4250 | 4236 | − 14 | 559 | 529 | − 30 |
| 26 | 4441 | 3691 | 3707 | + 16 | 468 | 465 | − 3 |
| 27 | 3810 | 3223 | 3242 | + 19 | 401 | 410 | + 9 |
| 28 | 3677 | 2822 | 2832 | + 10 | 387 | 358 | − 29 |
| 29 | 2622 | 2435 | 2474 | + 39 | 276 | 315 | + 39 |
| 30 | 2869 | 2159 | 2159 | 0 | 302 | 276 | − 26 |
| 31 | 1847 | 1857 | 1883 | + 26 | 194 | 242 | + 48 |
| 32 | 2076 | 1663 | 1641 | − 22 | 219 | 211 | − 8 |
| 33 | 1666 | 1444 | 1430 | − 14 | 175 | 185 | + 10 |
| 34 | 1508 | 1269 | 1245 | − 24 | 159 | 162 | + 3 |
| 35 | 1568 | 1110 | 1083 | − 27 | 165 | 142 | − 23 |
| 36 | 1243 | 945 | 941 | − 4 | 131 | 124 | − 7 |
| 37 | 944 | 814 | 817 | + 3 | 99 | 110 | + 11 |
| 38 | 1056 | 715 | 707 | − 8 | 111 | 96 | − 15 |
| 39 | 725 | 604 | 611 | + 7 | 77 | 87 | + 10 |
| 40 | 1040 | 527 | 524 | − 3 | 109 | 77 | − 32 |
| 41 | 607 | 418 | 447 | + 29 | 64 | 69 | + 5 |
| 42 | 816 | 354 | 378 | + 24 | 86 | 64 | − 18 |
| 43 | 734 | 268 | 314 | + 46 | 77 | 59 | − 18 |
| 44 | 1075 | 191 | 255 | + 69 | 113 | 54 | − 59 |
| 45 | 737 | 78 | 201 | +123 | 78 | 50 | − 28 |
| 46 | 88 | | | | | | |
| 47 | 86 | | | | | | |
| 48 | 78 | | | | | | |
| 49 | 45 | | | | | | |
| 50 & over. | 237 | | | | | | |

# TABLE XIV.

*Ages of Wisconsin and Iowa Volunteers.*

| Age at last birthday. | Number at each year of age. | Proportion at and over specified age. | | Difference. (C. — O.) | Proportion at each year of age. | | Difference. (C. — O.) |
|---|---|---|---|---|---|---|---|
| | | Observed. | Calculated. | | Observed. | Calculated. | |
| 13 | 11 | | | | | | |
| 14 | 22 | | | | | | |
| 15 | 79 | | | | | | |
| 16 | 369 | | | | | | |
| 17 | 829 | | | | | | |
| 18 | 11083 | 10000 | 10000 | 0 | 1485 | 1221 | −264 |
| 19 | 6440 | 8515 | 8779 | +264 | 863 | 1048 | +185 |
| 20 | 4874 | 7652 | 7731 | + 79 | 653 | 902 | +249 |
| 21 | 7082 | 6999 | 6829 | −170 | 949 | 778 | −171 |
| 22 | 5271 | 6050 | 6050 | 0 | 707 | 673 | − 34 |
| 23 | 4240 | 5343 | 5377 | + 34 | 569 | 585 | + 16 |
| 24 | 3718 | 4774 | 4792 | + 18 | 499 | 510 | + 11 |
| 25 | 3260 | 4275 | 4282 | + 7 | 437 | 447 | + 10 |
| 26 | 2953 | 3838 | 3835 | − 3 | 396 | 393 | − 3 |
| 27 | 2675 | 3442 | 3442 | 0 | 359 | 345 | − 14 |
| 28 | 2495 | 3083 | 3097 | + 14 | 334 | 310 | − 24 |
| 29 | 1844 | 2749 | 2787 | + 38 | 247 | 277 | + 30 |
| 30 | 1973 | 2502 | 2510 | + 8 | 264 | 250 | − 14 |
| 31 | 1472 | 2238 | 2260 | + 22 | 196 | 227 | + 31 |
| 32 | 1674 | 2042 | 2033 | − 9 | 224 | 207 | − 17 |
| 33 | 1432 | 1818 | 1826 | + 8 | 192 | 191 | − 1 |
| 34 | 1237 | 1626 | 1635 | + 9 | 166 | 177 | + 11 |
| 35 | 1359 | 1460 | 1458 | − 2 | 182 | 165 | − 17 |
| 36 | 1154 | 1278 | 1293 | + 15 | 155 | 155 | 0 |
| 37 | 1022 | 1123 | 1138 | + 15 | 137 | 146 | + 9 |
| 38 | 1104 | 986 | 992 | + 6 | 148 | 139 | − 9 |
| 39 | 873 | 838 | 853 | + 15 | 117 | 133 | + 16 |
| 40 | 967 | 721 | 720 | − 1 | 130 | 128 | − 2 |
| 41 | 670 | 591 | 592 | + 1 | 90 | 124 | + 34 |
| 42 | 886 | 501 | 468 | − 33 | 119 | 120 | + 1 |
| 43 | 950 | 382 | 348 | − 34 | 127 | 117 | − 10 |
| 44 | 1374 | 255 | 231 | − 24 | 184 | 114 | − 70 |
| 45 | 531 | 71 | 117 | + 46 | 71 | 112 | +`41 |
| 46 | 113 | | | | | | |
| 47 | 108 | | | | | | |
| 48 | 115 | | | . | | | |
| 49 | 76 | | | | | | |
| 50 & over. | 632 | | | | | | |

The agreement of these several special results with those deduced from their aggregate is remarkable. Only in one case, that of the Illinois troops, has the simple formula

$$s_n = a - b n + c h^n$$

failed to give all desired accordance between theory and observation ; and throughout the whole series the same peculiarities in the residuals are recognizable. In this connection I may add, what is in itself very significant, that attempts to deduce a law of distribution of age for troops recruited in Missouri, Kentucky, Tennessee, and Virginia have proved fruitless, and only small success was attainable for the Maryland volunteers. The inference is obvious, that the volunteering of troops from these States was not subject to the undisturbed influence of any statistical law. In the case of Illinois troops, a curious anomaly manifested itself in the residuals, namely, a cyclical or periodic term. This was found to be represented with sufficient accuracy by adding to the formula a term $d \sin \sqrt{n} \cdot 68°$, in which $d = 314$. I know of no satisfactory interpretation of this expression, but it has been used in the preparation of the table for that State.

In Table XV. is presented a summary of the results deduced from the special groups presented in Tables III. to XIV. All the constants are reduced to the same scale, and hold good for 10 000 troops of the ages 18 to 45 at last birthday, inclusive. The mean ages, as here given, refer, not to the last birthday, but to the actual date of enlistment.

The values of the constants for these special tables have been determined from a smaller number of equations of condition than were used for the grand total. In that each year was specially used ; in these the results were deduced from eight normal places.

## TABLE XV.

*Constants deduced for Special Classes of Volunteers.*

| Class. | Number of Soldiers | | Mean age at enlistment. | | $a.$ | $b.$ | $c.$ | $h.$ |
|---|---|---|---|---|---|---|---|---|
| | Of all ages. | Of military age. | For all. | For 18 to 45. | | | | |
| Total Enlisted Men | 1012273 | 996647 | 25.8362 | 25.8083 | 2102.8 | 77.04 | 7897.2 | 0.8536 |
| Total Infantry | 785120 | 773271 | 25.7827 | 25.7484 | 2080.0 | 75.84 | 7920.0 | 0.8514 |
| Total Cavalry | 117405 | 115951 | 25.8110 | 25.7795 | 1595.0 | 57.90 | 8405.0 | 0.8593 |
| Total Artillery | 42862 | 42357 | 26.1576 | 26.1202 | 2239.0 | 81.20 | 7761.0 | 0.8585 |
| Me., N.H., Vt., Conn. | 76445 | 75881 | 25.8792 | 25.8423 | 2112.0 | 73.06 | 7889.0 | 0.8514 |
| Massachusetts | 54705 | 54137 | 26.0561 | 26.0943 | 2016.0 | 76.40 | 7984.0 | 0.8662 |
| New York | 183281 | 181594 | 26.1308 | 26.1642 | 2390.5 | 88.86 | 7609.5 | 0.8575 |
| Pennsylvania | 116043 | 114844 | 25.8227 | 25.8331 | 2477.4 | 90.20 | 7523.0 | 0.8340 |
| Ohio | 153133 | 149936 | 25.4936 | 25.3859 | 2625.0 | 96.08 | 7375.0 | 0.8287 |
| Indiana | 70673 | 69536 | 24.7100 | 24.6858 | 1175.0 | 42.18 | 8825.0 | 0.8409 |
| Michigan | 39107 | 38489 | 25.5290 | 25.5276 | 1827.0 | 61.30 | 8173.0 | 0.8510 |
| Illinois | 96409 | 95003 | 25.9369 | 25.8935 | 2023.0 | 70.66 | 8057.0 | 0.8558 |
| Wisconsin and Iowa | 76987 | 74613 | 26.1571 | 25.9991 | 2737.0 | 100.20 | 7263.0 | 0.8456 |

In considering the residuals, the most striking feature is the excess of the recorded numbers at 18 and 21, which latter excess is counterbalanced by a deficiency at 20 and to some extent at 19 also. The explanation of this is readily found in the facts that enlistments of youths under 18 are not valid without the formal consent of parents, and that 21 is the period at which minority ceases. There can be no reasonable doubt that these residuals furnish the measure of the number under 18 and under 21, who misstated their age to the mustering officer. At the age of 18 the discordance is less marked than at 21, since the inducements to misstate operated near this age in different directions, many of those at 18 probably representing themselves as 21 years old, while their number was made good by others who untruly declared themselves as having completed their 18th year.

The excess of the recorded number at 21 averages $1\frac{4}{5}$ per cent., that deficiency at 20 is about 2 per cent., and at 19 about $1\frac{3}{5}$ per cent. The number recorded for 18 years is in excess by 1 per cent., although it varies very considerably in the different groups.

A large excess, representing the number of those who from similar motives understated their ages, is also to be seen at the age of 44 in most States, corresponding to an analogous deficiency at 45. This varies, however, in different States, owing in all probability to the different interpretation by the mustering officers of that provision of the law which precluded the acceptance of men over 45 years old. The average, in the more elaborately calculated table for the grand total, places the number at 44 in excess of the computed number by two thirds of its whole amount, and leaves that at 45 in defect by one fourth part.

For all other ages than those enumerated, the regular excess or defect of the residuals furnishes apparently the measure of the accuracy with which the ages were stated or recorded. It will be seen that at those ages which correspond to what are called round numbers, such as those divisible by 10, also, though to a less extent, at those divisible by 5, and in a still less but yet recognizable degree, at those divisible by 2, the recorded numbers are in excess; while the adjacent numbers, especially those ending in 1, 9, and 7, are in defect. The natural tendency which every one will recognize, and which inclines us to make use of certain more habitually employed numbers, rather than to use a minuteness repugnant to some persons, furnishes an adequate and, as I believe, the true explanation.

It will be readily noted that where any two of the above-named principles conflict, the residual is diminished; and that where they act in combination it is increased.

Lines showing the computed and the enrolled numbers of enlisted men are given on Chart *A*, and readily manifest these facts to the eye. The other data upon this chart are given for comparison, and will be referred to hereafter. It will be borne in mind that the numbers given do not, by a large amount, represent the actual numbers of enlisted volunteers or of volunteer officers, nor probably so much as two fifths of the total number of our soldiers in the struggle for national existence. They are relative quantities, deduced from only those data cited at the commencement of this paper, and illustrate, not the actual numbers for our troops, but the relative distribution of their ages.

The same results are presented in another form upon Chart *B*, which exhibits, for the enlisted men, the officers, and the white male population, the *proportion at and over the specified ages* and under 45 years, for each 10 000 men of military age.

Charts $C$ and $D$ show the law by which the ratios of officers and enlisted men to the white male population vary with the age. All the numbers are reduced to the scale of ten thousand of population at 18 years, Chart $C$ being constructed in reference to the whole United States, and Chart $D$ to the Loyal States only.

### 3. *Ages of Officers.*

The total number of officers of all ages is 37 184, that of those between 18 and 46 being 35 953.

On comparing the numbers at the several ages with the formula

$$s_n = a - bn + ch^n$$

we find at once that for certain ages the value of $h$ would be an impossible one; and that for other years, which would yield possible values, these values are so discordant and the residuals to which they lead become so large that it is manifest that the curve can be represented neither by this nor by any similar law.

Many trials have led to the empirical formula

$$s_n = a - bn^{k'} + c \sin n^k \theta \qquad (A)$$

as that which best represents the character of the curve. The extremely complicated manner, however, in which the six constants of this equation enter into the formula renders the attainment of a solution from six equations, by any direct process, a matter of great difficulty and inconvenience. Of course the constant $a$ represents the value of $s_n$ for $n = 0$, so that the problem really consists in the determination of the five quantities $b$, $c$, $k'$, $k$, and $\theta$. Graphic representations of the curve, by showing the points at which the third term becomes $= 0$, facilitated the approximate determination of these constants, and thus equations of condition were formed which have led to quite satisfactory values, giving an agreement between the formula and the observed numbers nearly if not quite as good as that obtained for the enlisted men by the formula already described.

Subsequently, investigations made for the purpose of extending this formula to the ages from 46 to 50 showed a deviation for these later years. This deviation seems only to be reconciled by the employment of an additional term containing two more constants, and the term thus found proves applicable to all ages above 30, essentially diminishing the residuals for all subsequent years.

The formula then stands for each 10 000 officers

$$s_n = 10\,000 - 736\,n^{0.75} + 1259 \sin n^{0.536} \times 45°.64 + 100 \sin (n - 12)\,18°$$

in which the last term is only to be employed for positive values of $n - 12$, that is, for ages above 30 years.

The near agreement of this formula with the observations will be recognized on Table XVI., which exhibits for each year of age from 18 to 50, as well as for those above 50, the actual and the proportionate observed number of officers, both at, and at and over, the given age, together with the corresponding numbers as deduced from the formula, and the discordances between Computation and Observation.

The dissimilarity of the curves thus found for officers and for enlisted men is most striking, as will be perceived by reference to Charts *A* and *B*. The chief discordance for the officers' curve is for the age of 18 years, at which, or at 19, the formula seems to fail. This is probably due in part to the fact that comparatively few officers were commissioned under the age of legal maturity, so that the law governing the distribution by age ought not to be regarded as applicable below 21 years.

# TABLE XVI.

## *Ages of Officers of United States Volunteers.*

| Age at last birthday. | Number at given age. | Proportion at given age | | | Number at and over given age. | Proportion at and over given age | | |
|---|---|---|---|---|---|---|---|---|
| | | Observed. | Calculated. | Difference. (C. — O.) | | Observed. | Calculated. | Difference. (C. — O.) |
| 13 | | | | | | | | |
| 14 | | | | | | | | |
| 15 | 1 | | | | 37183 | | | |
| 16 | 5 | | | | 37182 | | | |
| 17 | 5 | | | | 37177 | | | |
| 18 | 178 | 48 | −164 | −212 | 37172 | 10000 | 10000 | 0 |
| 19 | 409 | 110 | +233 | +123 | 37094 | 9952 | 10164 | +212 |
| 20 | 687 | 185 | 351 | +166 | 36685 | 9842 | 9931 | + 89 |
| 21 | 1630 | 439 | 443 | + 4 | 35998 | 9657 | 9580 | − 77 |
| 22 | 1839 | 495 | 500 | + 5 | 34368 | 9218 | 9137 | − 81 |
| 23 | 2101 | 565 | 537 | − 28 | 32529 | 8723 | 8637 | − 86 |
| 24 | 2234 | 601 | 557 | − 44 | 30428 | 8158 | 8100 | − 58 |
| 25 | 2161 | 581 | 567 | − 14 | 28194 | 7557 | 7543 | − 14 |
| 26 | 2114 | 569 | 563 | − 6 | 26033 | 6976 | 6976 | 0 |
| 27 | 1968 | 529 | 555 | + 26 | 23919 | 6407 | 6413 | + 6 |
| 28 | 2071 | 557 | 536 | − 21 | 21951 | 5878 | 5858 | − 20 |
| 29 | 1756 | 472 | 516 | + 44 | 19880 | 5321 | 5322 | + 1 |
| 30 | 1836 | 494 | 457 | − 37 | 18124 | 4849 | 4806 | − 43 |
| 31 | 1429 | 384 | 430 | + 46 | 16288 | 4355 | 4349 | − 6 |
| 32 | 1613 | 434 | 405 | − 29 | 14859 | 3971 | 3919 | − 52 |
| 33 | 1422 | 383 | 381 | − 2 | 13246 | 3537 | 3514 | − 23 |
| 34 | 1324 | 356 | 359 | + 3 | 11824 | 3154 | 3133 | − 21 |
| 35 | 1434 | 386 | 335 | − 51 | 10500 | 2798 | 2774 | − 24 |
| 36 | 1221 | 328 | 313 | − 15 | 9066 | 2412 | 2439 | + 27 |
| 37 | 1031 | 277 | 291 | + 14 | 7845 | 2084 | 2126 | + 42 |
| 38 | 1033 | 278 | 269 | − 9 | 6814 | 1807 | 1835 | + 28 |
| 39 | 813 | 219 | 245 | + 26 | 5781 | 1529 | 1566 | + 37 |
| 40 | 874 | 235 | 222 | − 13 | 4968 | 1310 | 1321 | + 11 |
| 41 | 557 | 149 | 197 | + 48 | 4094 | 1075 | 1099 | + 24 |
| 42 | 656 | 176 | 171 | − 5 | 3537 | 926 | 902 | − 24 |
| 43 | 485 | 130 | 148 | + 18 | 2881 | 750 | 731 | − 19 |
| 44 | 598 | 161 | 124 | − 37 | 2396 | 620 | 583 | − 37 |
| 45 | 478 | 130 | 100 | − 30 | 1798 | 459 | 459 | 0 |
| 46 | 217 | 58 | 86 | + 28 | 1320 | 329 | 359 | + 30 |
| 47 | 184 | 50 | 70 | + 20 | 1103 | 271 | 273 | + 2 |
| 48 | 175 | 47 | 58 | + 11 | 919 | 221 | 203 | − 18 |
| 49 | 121 | 33 | 55 | + 22 | 744 | 174 | 145 | − 29 |
| 50 & over. | 523 | 141 | 90 | − 51 | 523 | 141 | 90 | − 51 |

The mean age at last birthday for all the officers is . 3̇0̇.4406

"     "     "     for those between 18 & 45   29.8338

and the mean age of the mean at last birthday is . 29.45

or about 29.94 at the time of their muster into the service. Above and below this age the number of officers was equal.

The annexed Table XVII. exhibits the relative proportions of officers to the enlisted men, and of these to the white male population of the whole United States and of the Loyal States respectively, as given by the census of 1860, taken less than one year before the call to arms.

The caution must here be repeated, that the " proportion of enlisted men to the population," as here given, does not at all apply to the armies of the nation during the rebellion. It relates solely to the number of volunteer troops here considered; and this Table XVII. is presented solely to make manifest the laws according to which the ratios of enlisted men to the population, and the ratios of officers to men, varied with the age.

## T A B L E   X V I I.

### Relative Proportions
### of Officers, Enlisted Men, and White Male Population,
### for the first million of Volunteers.

| AGE. | Proportion of Officers to Enlisted Men. | Proportion of Enlisted Men to Population of U. States. | Proportion of Enlisted Men to Population of Loyal States. | AGE. | Proportion of Officers to Enlisted Men. | Proportion of Enlisted Men to Population of U. States. | Proportion of Enlisted Men to Population of Loyal States. |
|---|---|---|---|---|---|---|---|
| 18 | 0.001 | 0.448 | 0.570 | 32 | 0.072 | 0.100 | 0.123 |
| 19 | 0.007 | 0.393 | 0.502 | 33 | 0.074 | 0.093 | 0.119 |
| 20 | 0.013 | 0.345 | 0.442 | 34 | 0.076 | 0.088 | 0.112 |
| 21 | 0.019 | 0.305 | 0.391 | 35 | 0.077 | 0.084 | 0.105 |
| 22 | 0.025 | 0.269 | 0.363 | 36 | 0.078 | 0.080 | 0.100 |
| 23 | 0.031 | 0.239 | 0.308 | 37 | 0.077 | 0.077 | 0.096 |
| 24 | 0.037 | 0.212 | 0.275 | 38 | 0.075 | 0.075 | 0.093 |
| 25 | 0.043 | 0.190 | 0.246 | 39 | 0.073 | 0.074 | 0.090 |
| 26 | 0.048 | 0.170 | 0.221 | 40 | 0.068 | 0.073 | 0.088 |
| 27 | 0.054 | 0.154 | 0.199 | 41 | 0.062 | 0.073 | 0.088 |
| 28 | 0.059 | 0.139 | 0.180 | 42 | 0.057 | 0.073 | 0.087 |
| 29 | 0.063 | 0.127 | 0.164 | 43 | 0.049 | 0.074 | 0.087 |
| 30 | 0.065 | 0.116 | 0.150 | 44 | 0.041 | 0.075 | 0.088 |
| 31 | 0.068 | 0.107 | 0.138 | 45 | 0.033 | 0.076 | 0.089 |

#### 4. *Population of the United States and of the Loyal States.*

The great and unexpected dissimilarity between the law of distribution of age for officers and for men led, as I have already mentioned, to an investigation of the ages of the white male population, both of the whole United States, and of the Loyal States considered by themselves. And, in the absence of any distinct criterion, those States which were free from slavery in 1860, together with Delaware, Maryland, Kentucky, and Missouri, have been classed as Loyal States. The territory of West Virginia, eastern Tennessee, &c., is thus excluded, although inhabited by a thoroughly loyal population, which contributed about twenty of the regiments here computed; and about ten other regiments, included in our data, were raised in States not accounted loyal. But all these are offset by the very considerable portion of the inhabitants of the four Slave States above named, from which the insurgent army was reinforced.

The only materials available for the inquiry are contained in the tables, derived from the official census of the United States in 1860. Of course it is the male population alone which has any relation to the present research.

The difficulty of deducing from these meagre details the number of males at each year of military age is apparent at the first glance. Had the classification between the ages of 20 and 50 been in six groups of five years each, instead of three groups of ten years, the facility and accuracy of the investigation would have been incomparably greater. As it is, the only available data are contained in the second column of the following tables, XVIII. and XIX. These tables give, in column 9, the results of the formulas obtained for representing the observed numbers given in column 2. The degree of correctness of these formulas may be estimated by means of column 4, which shows the excess of the calculated number over the number given by the census, in decimals of the latter. The accordance for ages above 20 years is remarkably good. Beyond 50 years the agreement is not so close as between 20 and 50, but is nevertheless quite tolerable; but the comparison is omitted here as not pertinent to the subject, since none of the census-numbers for groups of ages above 50 have been employed in the computation.

The other columns require no explanation. It will be remembered that the numbers of enlisted men and officers here given are merely those belonging to the original volunteer regiments at the time of their enlistment, excluding all recruits, substitutes, drafted men, &c. Also, that the numbers apply only to those regiments which had been mustered into the United States service prior to the collection of our data, as shown on page 2.

## TABLE XVIII.

*White Male Population of the United States in 1860.*

Comparison between Computed and Observed Ages.

| Age at last birthday. | White Male Population of the United States. | | Difference. (C. — O.) | Enlisted Men of first volunteers. | Officers of first volunteers. | Ratio to White Male Population. | |
|---|---|---|---|---|---|---|---|
| | Census. | Computed. | | | | Men. | Officers. |
| 10 — 15 | 1 578 274 | 1 547 730 | —0.0193 | | | | |
| 15 — 20 | 1 391 950 | 1 422 340 | +0.0245 | | | | |
| 18 — 20 | | 553 360 | | 219 200 | 587 | 0.395 | 0.0011 |
| 20 — 30 | 2 465 276 | 2 436 770 | —0.0116 | 529 809 | 18 561 | 0.217 | 0.0076 |
| 30 — 40 | 1 847 259 | 1 847 810 | 0.0000 | 165 292 | 13 156 | 0.090 | 0.0071 |
| 40 — 45 | | 807 860 | | 63 667 | | 0.079 | |
| 40 — 50 | 1 215 031 | 1 216 690 | +0.0014 | | 4 868 | | 0.0040 |
| 18 — 45 | | 5 645 800 | | 977 968 | | | |

## TABLE XIX.

*White Male Population of the Loyal States in 1860.*

Comparison between Computed and Observed Ages.

| Age at last birthday. | White Male Population of the Loyal States. | | Difference. (C. — O.) | Enlisted Men of first volunteers. | Officers of first volunteers. | Ratio to White Male Population. | |
|---|---|---|---|---|---|---|---|
| | Census. | Computed. | | | | Men. | Officers. |
| 10 — 15 | 1 211 521 | 1 179 260 | —0.0266 | | | | |
| 15 — 20 | 1 095 934 | 1 110 770 | +0.0135 | | | | |
| 18 — 20 | | 435 100 | | 219 200 | 587 | 0.502 | 0.0014 |
| 20 — 30 | 1 971 486 | 1 956 890 | —0.0075 | 529 809 | 18 561 | 0.271 | 0.0095 |
| 30 — 40 | 1 517 736 | 1 517 720 | 0.0000 | 165 292 | 13 156 | 0.109 | 0.0087 |
| 40 — 45 | • | 664 510 | | 63 667 | | 0.096 | |
| 40 — 50 | 996 481 | 996 350 | 0.0000 | | 4 868 | | 0.0049 |
| 18 — 45 | | 4 574 220 | | 977 968 | | | |

The formulas which thus represent the number of white males from the age of 10 years upwards are, —

for the United States

$$x = 445\,440 \sin (134° \ 34' + (y-10) \cdot 52')$$

for the Loyal States

$$x = 257\,870 \sin (111° \ 6'.1 + (y-10) \cdot 80'.2)$$

in which $x$ is the number at the year of age $y$.

Assuming these values to be correct, we find the distribution of the white male population in 1860 to have been as represented in Tables XX. and XXI.

These tables show, for the United States and the Loyal States respectively, the actual numbers : — first, at each year of age from 15 to 50, inclusive ; secondly, at and over each year of age from 15 to 50, inclusive ; thirdly, at and over each year within the limits of military age from 18 upwards, and also the corresponding relative or proportional numbers, using those for 18 years as the units.

Subsequent investigation has led to the detection of a formula totally different in structure from those above given, but which, although its agreement with the census-numbers within the years of military age is by no means so close as these afford, yet represents the various censuses of the United States and those of foreign countries throughout the period of human life with a degree of precision never before attained, so far as I am aware. It represents the number of infants under one year as well as, and indeed better than, the number at middle life or advanced years ; and I cannot avoid the conviction that this formula affords an important step toward the true mathematical expression of what we may call the life-curve. Modifications will doubtless be made in it ; indeed, it manifestly gives the numbers too small for the ages under 5 years, over 70 years, and between 20 and 45 years, while those of later childhood and youth on the one side, and of advanced maturity on the other, are in excess. But the discordances are small, and I hardly think that any expression of equal simplicity will be found which will represent the life-curve more closely.

Of this formula, which is simply

$$s_n = a \sin n \, k^n \, \theta$$

where $s_n$ represents the sum of all under the age $n$, $a$ is the total number, and $k$, $\theta$ are two constants characteristic of the especial population under examination, details and applications are given in the Appendix ; where also are tables exhibiting the distribution of the total white male population of the United States and of the Loyal States, as given by this law. The values differ slightly from those in Tables XXI. and XXII., which, for the census of 1860 at least, seem to be more accurate within the limits to which they are extended, although the corresponding numbers beyond these limits would be less accordant with observation.

5

## TABLE XX.

### *White Male Population of the United States in 1860.*

| Age at last birthday. | Actual Number | | | Relative Number | | |
|---|---|---|---|---|---|---|
| | At the given age. | At and over given age. | At and over given age and under 46. | At the given age. | At and over given age. | At and over given age & under 46. |
| 15 | 294 770 | 8 252 612 | | | | |
| 16 | 289 680 | 7 957 842 | | | | |
| 17 | 284 530 | 7 668 162 | | | | |
| 18 | 279 320 | 7 383 632 | 5 645 800 | 10 000 | 10 000 | 10 000 |
| 19 | 274 040 | 7 104 312 | 5 366 480 | 9 811 | 9 622 | 9 505 |
| 20 | 268 700 | 6 830 272 | 5 092 440 | 9 620 | 9 251 | 9 020 |
| 21 | 263 290 | 6 561 572 | 4 823 740 | 9 426 | 8 887 | 8 544 |
| 22 | 257 820 | 6 298 282 | 4 560 450 | 9 230 | 8 530 | 8 078 |
| 23 | 252 300 | 6 040 462 | 4 302 630 | 9 033 | 8 181 | 7 621 |
| 24 | 246 720 | 5 788 162 | 4 050 330 | 8 833 | 7 839 | 7 174 |
| 25 | 241 090 | 5 541 442 | 3 803 610 | 8 631 | 7 505 | 6 737 |
| 26 | 235 380 | 5 300 352 | 3 562 520 | 8 427 | 7 179 | 6 310 |
| 27 | 229 640 | 5 064 972 | 3 327 140 | 8 222 | 6 860 | 5 893 |
| 28 | 223 840 | 4 835 332 | 3 097 500 | 8 014 | 6 549 | 5 486 |
| 29 | 217 990 | 4 611 492 | 2 873 660 | 7 804 | 6 246 | 5 090 |
| 30 | 212 090 | 4 393 502 | 2 655 670 | 7 593 | 5 951 | 4 704 |
| 31 | 206 140 | 4 181 412 | 2 443 580 | 7 380 | 5 664 | 4 328 |
| 32 | 200 140 | 3 975 272 | 2 237 440 | 7 165 | 5 385 | 3 963 |
| 33 | 194 100 | 3 775 132 | 2 037 300 | 6 949 | 5 114 | 3 609 |
| 34 | 188 020 | 3 581 032 | 1 843 200 | 6 731 | 4 851 | 3 265 |
| 35 | 181 890 | 3 393 012 | 1 655 180 | 6 512 | 4 596 | 2 932 |
| 36 | 175 710 | 3 211 122 | 1 473 290 | 6 291 | 4 350 | 2 610 |
| 37 | 169 500 | 3 035 412 | 1 297 580 | 6 068 | 4 112 | 2 299 |
| 38 | 163 250 | 2 865 912 | 1 128 080 | 5 845 | 3 882 | 1 999 |
| 39 | 156 970 | 2 702 662 | 964 830 | 5 620 | 3 661 | 1 710 |
| 40 | 150 640 | 2 545 692 | 807 860 | 5 393 | 3 448 | 1 432 |
| 41 | 144 290 | 2 395 052 | 657 220 | 5 166 | 3 244 | 1 165 |
| 42 | 137 900 | 2 250 762 | 512 930 | 4 937 | 3 049 | 909 |
| 43 | 131 470 | 2 112 862 | 375 030 | 4 707 | 2 862 | 665 |
| 44 | 125 020 | 1 981 392 | 243 560 | 4 476 | 2 684 | 432 |
| 45 | 118 540 | 1 856 372 | 118 540 | 4 244 | 2 515 | 210 |
| 46 | 112 030 | 1 737 832 | | 4 011 | 2 354 | |
| 47 | 105 500 | 1 625 802 | | 3 777 | 2 202 | |
| 48 | 98 940 | 1 520 302 | | 3 542 | 2 059 | |
| 49 | 92 360 | 1 421 362 | | 3 307 | 1 925 | |
| 50 | 85 760 | 1 329 002 | | 3 072 | 1 800 | |

# TABLE XXI.

## White Male Population of the Loyal States in 1860.

| Age at last birth-day. | Actual Number | | | Relative Number | | | Prop. to W. Male Pop. of United States. |
|---|---|---|---|---|---|---|---|
| | At the given age. | At and over given age. | At and over given age and under 46. | At the given age. | At and over given age. | At and over given age & under 46. | |
| 15 | 228 120 | 6 675 533 | | | | | 7 739 |
| 16 | 225 270 | 6 447 413 | | | | | 7 776 |
| 17 | 222 280 | 6 222 143 | | | | | 7 812 |
| 18 | 219 160 | 5 999 863 | 4 574 220 | 10 000 | 10 000 | 10 000 | 7 846 |
| 19 | 215 940 | 5 780 703 | 4 355 060 | 9 853 | 9 634 | 9 521 | 7 880 |
| 20 | 212 600 | 5 564 763 | 4 139 120 | 9 700 | 9 275 | 9 049 | 7 912 |
| 21 | 209 130 | 5 352 163 | 3 926 520 | 9 542 | 8 920 | 8 584 | 7 943 |
| 22 | 205 550 | 5 143 033 | 3 717 390 | 9 379 | 8 572 | 8 127 | 7 973 |
| 23 | 201 870 | 4 937 483 | 3 511 840 | 9 211 | 8 229 | 7 678 | 8 001 |
| 24 | 198 070 | 4 735 613 | 3 309 970 | 9 038 | 7 893 | 7 237 | 8 028 |
| 25 | 194 160 | 4 537 543 | 3 111 900 | 8 859 | 7 563 | 6 804 | 8 054 |
| 26 | 190 150 | 4 343 383 | 2 917 740 | 8 676 | 7 239 | 6 379 | 8 078 |
| 27 | 186 040 | 4 153 233 | 2 727 590 | 8 488 | 6 922 | 5 963 | 8 101 |
| 28 | 181 820 | 3 967 193 | 2 541 550 | 8 296 | 6 612 | 5 555 | 8 123 |
| 29 | 177 500 | 3 785 373 | 2 359 730 | 8 099 | 6 309 | 5 157 | 8 141 |
| 30 | 173 100 | 3 607 873 | 2 182 230 | 7 898 | 6 013 | 4 769 | 8 162 |
| 31 | 168 590 | 3 434 773 | 2 009 130 | 7 692 | 5 725 | 4 391 | 8 179 |
| 32 | 163 990 | 3 266 183 | 1 840 540 | 7 483 | 5 444 | 4 022 | 8 194 |
| 33 | 159 300 | 3 102 193 | 1 676 550 | 7 269 | 5 170 | 3 663 | 8 207 |
| 34 | 154 530 | 2 942 893 | 1 517 250 | 7 051 | 4 905 | 3 315 | 8 219 |
| 35 | 149 680 | 2 788 363 | 1 362 720 | 6 829 | 4 647 | 2 977 | 8 229 |
| 36 | 144 730 | 2 638 683 | 1 213 040 | 6 604 | 4 398 | 2 650 | 8 237 |
| 37 | 139 720 | 2 493 953 | 1 068 310 | 6 375 | 4 157 | 2 334 | 8 243 |
| 38 | 134 620 | 2 354 233 | 928 590 | 6 143 | 3 924 | 2 029 | 8 246 |
| 39 | 129 460 | 2 219 613 | 793 970 | 5 907 | 3 699 | 1 735 | 8 247 |
| 40 | 124 230 | 2 090 153 | 664 510 | 5 668 | 3 484 | 1 452 | 8 247 |
| 41 | 118 920 | 1 965 923 | 540 280 | 5 426 | 3 277 | 1 180 | 8 242 |
| 42 | 113 550 | 1 847 003 | 421 360 | 5 181 | 3 078 | 920 | 8 234 |
| 43 | 108 110 | 1 733 453 | 307 810 | 4 933 | 2 889 | 672 | 8 223 |
| 44 | 102 620 | 1 625 343 | 199 700 | 4 683 | 2 709 | 436 | 8 209 |
| 45 | 97 080 | 1 522 723 | 97 080 | 4 430 | 2 538 | 212 | 8 190 |
| 46 | 91 480 | 1 425 643 | | 4 174 | 2 376 | | 8 165 |
| 47 | 85 830 | 1 334 163 | | 3 916 | 2 224 | | 8 136 |
| 48 | 80 130 | 1 248 333 | | 3 656 | 2 081 | | 8 099 |
| 49 | 74 400 | 1 168 203 | | 3 394 | 1 947 | | 8 055 |
| 50 | 68 640 | 1 093 803 | | 3 130 | 1 823 | | 8 001 |

The results present some curious contrasts between the life-curves for the total population in the loyal States and in the insurgent States, which may be best recognized by reference to the appended chart, marked $E$. This chart exhibits the number of white males at each year of age from 18 to 50, corresponding to each 10 000 at the age of 18. It will be seen at once that the curvature of the line representing the population of the insurgent States is in the direction opposite to that of the lines belonging to the loyal States and to the whole country. The dotted line is straight, and shows what the distribution would be, did it follow a regular arithmetical progression. To what extent this difference may be due to immigration from Europe, which has been chiefly to the Free States, I will not undertake to estimate. We have seen, however, that the law of distribution of our volunteer troops according to ages was essentially the same for those States to which immigration is · greatest as for those to which it is least.

----

The construction of all the curves laid down on the accompanying charts will be manifest without explanation. For those ordinates which belong to the respective ages they give the corresponding numbers.

# APPENDIX.

## ON THE AGES OF A POPULATION.

In the course of the preceding investigation, the interesting question as to the general distribution of a population by ages became prominent; and the inquiry continually suggested itself, how far any simple formula might be capable of representing the observed numbers for all ages of life. This has incidentally led to the detection of what seems to be the true law, which, although not strictly pertaining to the subject in hand, seems yet to possess sufficient practical value and importance in its indirect bearing to justify its introduction here, — the more especially, since endeavors to obtain information on this point elsewhere have proved fruitless.

It appears that, in a population at all homogeneous in its character, the number of persons under the age $n$ years may be represented by the simple expression

$$N = a \sin n\, k^n\, \theta$$

in which $a$ denotes the total number of the population, while $k$ and $\theta$ are constants peculiar to the country and epoch. The quantity $\theta$ is an angle somewhat larger than $1°$, and $k$ is a number, generally a little less than unity.

For the special case $k = 1$, the formula becomes

$$N = a \sin n\, \theta$$

containing only one unknown quantity, the angle $\theta$, to be determined by investigation.

A very peculiar characteristic of this law is recognizable in the circumstance that the number at any given age appears to be strictly proportional to the whole population; so that the expectation of life, for the average individual, is as well represented as is the general distribution by ages of the total number of individuals, of whom the population is composed.

Investigating the values of the constants $k$ and $\theta$ for the people of the United States at each of the last four enumerations, we find

| Date | $k$ | $\theta$ |
|------|--------|----------|
| 1830 | 0.9918 | 2°.0524 |
| 1840 | 0.9921 | 1°.9747 |
| 1850 | 0.9932 | 1°.8361 |
| 1860 | 0.9941 | 1°.7307. |

The census of 1820 is not sufficiently distinct, in the assortment by ages, to permit a determination of the constants, but the indications are clear that a proper enumeration would have afforded results in conformity with the preceding series; the value of $k$ being smaller, and that of $\theta$ larger than for the population in 1830.

The curious fact thus becomes evident, that our population has, during the last forty years or more, been gradually assimilating itself to the normal type represented by $k = 1$; growing, or developing itself, so to speak, toward a compliance with the simple law

$$N = a \sin n\theta$$

in which the value of $\theta$ indicates the longevity of the people, since, according to the formula, the entire population becomes extinct at the age when $n\theta = 90°$.

How far immigration has affected the values of the constants for the United States we will not now inquire. Were the tendency to immigrate independent of age, no appreciable influence could be traced to this source; and the character of the immigration into this country seems to have been such as to exhibit no great preponderance or deficiency for any one period of life, except perhaps that there is some deficiency in the relative number at the most advanced ages. But the accessions to our population from Ireland and Germany appear to have been in most cases by families, and not composed chiefly of persons in the prime of life or fullness of strength, as is the case in very new countries.

The English people appearing to afford a fair specimen of a permanent and normal population, the last two censuses of England and Wales were examined, and with the following result: —

| Date | $k$ | $\theta$ |
|------|--------|----------|
| 1851 | 0.9957 | 1°.4702 |
| 1861 | 0.9962 | 1°.4316. |

Thus a similar phenomenon is manifested by the English enumerations to that exhibited by the American census-returns; the values of $k$ approaching unity, and those of $\theta$ diminishing. The smaller value of the angle $\theta$

indicates a longer duration of life in that country ; but $k$, the modulus of the change by geometric progression, was not larger for England in 1851 than it bids fair to be for the United States in ten years from the present time.

Passing next to the French population, we find the value $k = 1$ as the result alike of the last three enumerations, the values of $\theta$ being

| | |
|---|---|
| in 1851 | 1°.0553 |
| " 1856 | 1°.0556 |
| " 1861 | 1°.0473. |

The remarkable peculiarity of the life-curve for France, as regards the small infantile mortality, is well exhibited by the chart $F$, which shows the number living, at each year of age, for every million in the population. The several curves of this chart represent the distribution of ages for the United States in 1830 and 1860, (those for the intermediate decades being omitted to avoid confusion,) for England in 1861, and for France. The English curve for 1851 would differ too slightly from that for 1861 to be conveniently distinguished on the chart ; and the French curves for 1851, 1856, and 1861 would be undistinguishable from one another.

The chart $G$ shows the corresponding values of $N$, (the number under each year of age,) for each nation, and clearly manifests the differences in the law, corresponding to the diversity in the constants.

The tables of population deduced from the census-returns already cited, together with the values given by the formula, are here appended, reduced however, in each case, to the scale of one million of population. The differences are given in decimals of the census-numbers, and the accordance between the formula and the recorded numbers will be manifest at the first inspection. The chief discrepancies will be found in the French tables, for the ages

| | | | | | |
|---|---|---|---|---|---|
| exceeding 50, | in the census of | | | | 1851 |
| " 55, | " | " | " | " | 1856 |
| " 60, | " | " | " | " | 1861. |

This curious circumstance and the nature of the discordances suggest some historical explanation ; which the disturbed condition of the French nation at the period corresponding to the birth of this portion of the population seems to render plausible.

## TABLE XXII.

*Ages of the Population of the United States,*
*as deduced from the Census Returns of* 1830 *and* 1840.

| AGE. | Census of 1830. | | | Census of 1840. | | |
|---|---|---|---|---|---|---|
| | Proportional numbers. | | Difference. (C. — O.) | Proportional numbers. | | Difference. (C. — O.) |
| | Observed. | Calculated. | | Observed. | Calculated. | |
| 0 — 5 | 17977 | 17082 | ' —0.050 | 17437 | 16334 | —0.063 |
| 5 — 10 | 14576 | 15254 | +0.046 | 14173 | 14651 | +0.034 |
| 10 — 15 | 12452 | 13280 | +0.014 | 12094 | 12931 | +0.069 |
| 15 — 20 | 11147 | 11318 | +0.024 | 10911 | ♂ 11205 | +0.027 |
| 20 — 30 | 17752 | 17244 | —0.029 | 18155 | 17456 | —0.038 |
| 30 — 40 | 10908 | 11287 | +0.035 | 11597 | 11790 | +0.017 |
| 40 — 50 | 6886 | 6932 | +0.007 | 7320 | 7466 | +0.020 |
| 50 — 60 | 4308 | 3973 | —0.078 | 4365 | 4389 | +0.005 |
| 60 — 70 | 2525 | 2100 | —0.168 | 2449 | 2343 | —0.043 |
| 70 — 80 | 1104 | 992 | —0.100 | 1132 | 1067 | —0.058 |
| 80 & over | 365 | 540 | | 367 | 368 | |

## TABLE XXIII.

*Ages of the Population of the United States,*
*as deduced from the Census Returns of* 1850 *and* 1860.

| AGE. | Census of 1850. | | | Census of 1860. | | |
|---|---|---|---|---|---|---|
| | Proportional numbers. | | Difference. (C. — O.) | Proportional numbers. | | Difference. (C. — O.) |
| | Observed. | Calculated. | | Observed. | Calculated. | |
| 0 — 1 | 2751 | 3170 | +0.152 | 2998 | 3003 | +0.002 |
| 1 — 5 | 12070 | 12215 | +0.012 | 12300 | 11608 | —0.056 |
| 5 — 10 | 13836 | 14102 | +0.019 | 13117 | 13484 | +0.028 |
| 10 — 15 | 12292 | 12564 | +0.022 | 11588 | 12206 | +0.053 |
| 15 — 20 | 10892 | 10990 | +0.009 | 10625 | 10853 | +0.021 |
| 20 — 30 | 18562 | 17505 | —0.057 | 18242 | 17692 | —0.030 |
| 30 — 40 | 12368 | 12225 | —0.012 | 13012 | 12760 | —0.019 |
| 40 — 50 | 8130 | 8019 | —0.013 | 8496 | 8618 | +0.014 |
| 50 — 60 | 4903 | 4883 | —0.041 | 5214 | 5366 | +0.029 |
| 60 — 70 | 2667 | 2695 | +0.010 | 2910 | 2953 | +0.015 |
| 70 — 80 | 1147 | 1250 | +0.090 | 1158 | 1261 | +0.089 |
| 80 & over | 382 | 382 | | 340 | 196 | |

# TABLE XXIV.

*Ages of the Population of England and Wales,*
*as deduced from the Census Returns of* 1851 *and* 1861.

| AGE. | Census of 1851. | | | Census of 1861. | | |
|---|---|---|---|---|---|---|
| | Proportional numbers. | | Difference. (C. — O.) | Proportional numbers. | | Difference. (C. — O.) |
| | Observed | Calculated. | | Observed. | Calculated. | |
| 0 — 5 | 13006 | 12533 | −0.035 | 13352 | 12245 | −0.083 |
| 5 — 10 | 11590 | 11800 | +0.018 | 11588 | 11575 | −0.001 |
| 10 — 15 | 10616 | 10987 | +0.034 | 10415 | 10819 | +0.040 |
| 15 — 20 | 9832 | 10079 | +0.013 | 9688 | 10007 | +0.032 |
| 20 — 25 | 9441 | 9114 | −0.036 | 9317 | 9108 | −0.023 |
| 25 — 30 | 8307 | 8170 | −0.017 | 7932 | 8178 | +0.030 |
| 30 — 35 | 7168 | 7179 | +0.004 | 6950 | 7282 | +0.046 |
| 35 — 40 | 6083 | 7273 | +0.030 | 6111 | 6352 | +0.038 |
| 40 — 45 | 5393 | 5378 | −0.003 | 5638 | 5506 | −0.024 |
| 45 — 50 | 4440 | 4546 | +0.023 | 4617 | 4705 | +0.019 |
| 50 — 55 | 3934 | 3782 | −0.040 | 3995 | 3820 | −0.046 |
| 55 — 60 | 2919 | 3061 | +0.046 | 3039 | 3245 | +0.063 |
| 60 — 65 | 2668 | 2426 | −0.100 | 2751 | 2512 | −0.095 |
| 65 — 70 | 1815 | 1841 | +0.014 | 1862 | 1910 | +0.025 |
| 70 — 75 | 1386 | 1332 | −0.041 | 1391 | 1355 | −0.026 |
| 75 — 80 | 809 | 876 | +0.076 | 794 | 869 | +0.086 |
| 80 — 85 | 410 · | 481 | +0.173 | 394 | 435 | +0.104 |
| 85 & over. | 183 | 142 | | 146 | 77 | |
| Total, | 100000 | 100000 | | 100000 | 100000 | |

## FORMULAS

For 1851, $N = 100\,000 \sin n \, (0.99575)^n \, . \, 1°.4702.$

1861, $N = 100\,000 \sin n \, (0.99616)^n \, . \, 1°.4316.$

6

# TABLE XXV.

*Ages of the Population of France,*

*as deduced from the Census Returns of* 1851, 1856, *and* 1861.

| AGE. | Census of 1851. | | | Census of 1856. | | | Census of 1861. | | |
|---|---|---|---|---|---|---|---|---|---|
| | Proportional numbers. | | Difference. (C. — O.) | Proportional numbers. | | Difference. (C. — O.) | Proportional numbers. | | Difference. (C. — O.) |
| | Ob-served. | Calcu-lated. | | Ob-served. | Calcu-lated. | | Ob-served. | Calcu-lated. | |
| 0 — 5 | 9291 | 9208 | −0.009 | 9568 | 9200 | −0.038 | 9677 | 9124 | −0.088 |
| 5 — 10 | 9216 | 9130 | −0.009 | 9120 | 9119 | 0.000 | 8767 | 9052 | +0.032 |
| 10 — 15 | 8800 | 8946 | +0.016 | 8821 | 8965 | +0.016 | 8668 | 8898 | +0.027 |
| 15 — 20 | 8805 | 8716 | −0.010 | 8530 | 8736 | +0.024 | 8701 | 8722 | +0.002 |
| 20 — 25 | 8326 | 8437 | +0.013 | 8077 | 8427 | +0.043 | 8237 | 8374 | +0.017 |
| 25 — 30 | 8020 | 8036 | +0.002 | 8075 | 8051 | −0.003 | 7857 | 8005 | +0.019 |
| 30 — 35 | 7565 | 7616 | +0.007 | 7575 | 7614 | +0.005 | 7421 | 7564 | +0.019 |
| 35 — 40 | 7188 | 7105 | −0.012 | 7255 | 7092 | −0.022 | 7098 | 7071 | −0.004 |
| 40 — 45 | 6596 | 6534 | −0.009 | 6656 | 6526 | −0.020 | 6625 | 6514 | −0.017 |
| 45 — 50 | 5869 | 5890 | +0.004 | 6041 | 5902 | −0.023 | 6155 | 5900 | −0.041 |
| 50 — 55 | 5782 | 5233 | −0.095 | 5317 | 5228 | −0.017 | 5382 | 5254 | −0.024 |
| 55 — 60 | 4390 | 4512 | +0.028 | 4838 | 4503 | −0.069 | 4559 | 4518 | −0.009 |
| 60 — 65 | 3670 | 3753 | +0.023 | 3734 | 3753 | +0.005 | 4160 | 3790 | −0.090 |
| 65 — 70 | 2785 | 2954 | +0.059 | 2757 | 2958 | +0.076 | 2941 | 3016 | +0.025 |
| 70 — 75 | 1952 | 2148 | +0.100 | 1902 | 2145 | +0.128 | 1940 | 2218 | +0.143 |
| 75 — 80 | 1062 | 1313 | +0.239 | 1088 | 1312 | +0.205 | 1123 | 1398 | +0.245 |
| 80 — 85 | 480 | 468 | −0.025 | 453 | 468 | −0.033 | .490 | 568 | +0.159 |
| 85 & over. | 203 | 1 | | 193 | 1 | | 199 | 14 | |
| Total, | 100000 | 100000 | | 100000 | 100000 | | 100000 | 100000 | |

## FORMULAS

For 1851,     $N = 100\,000 \sin n\,(1°.0553).$

1856,     $N = 100\,000 \sin n\,(1°.0556).$

1861,     $N = 100\,000 \sin n\,(1°.0473).$

The agreement of the observed numbers with those given by our formula is indicated by the quantities in the columns headed $C. — O.$ (i. e. Computed *minus* Observed), and appears to be entirely within the limits of probable error in the enumeration, — if we except those discordances for the French census already alluded to. It affords a strong argument for belief that the true form of the normal life-curve is closely represented by the sine-formula.

The only other statistics of ages for European populations, which have been conveniently accessible, are contained in the abstract of the Prussian census of 1852, given by Brachelli, in the second volume of his *Deutsche Staatenkunde.* A discussion of the numbers there recorded gives

$$k = 0.9960, \qquad \theta = 1°.4702,$$

these values being closely similar to those for England and Wales in 1851.

It is manifest that if the number under any given age $n$ be represented by the expression

$$N = a \sin n\, k^n\, \theta$$

the number between the ages $n$ and $n+1$ will be expressed by

$$2a \sin \tfrac{1}{2} k^n (kn + k - n)\theta. \ \cos \tfrac{1}{2} k^n (kn + k + n)\theta,$$

and the mortality at the same period, by the finite difference of this quantity.

But when $\theta$ becomes unity, these values are greatly simplified, and we have

Population under the age $n$ years $= a \sin n\theta$

Population at  "   "   "   "   $= 2a \sin \tfrac{1}{2}\theta \cos (n + \tfrac{1}{2})\theta$

Mortality  "   "   "   "   "   $= 4a \sin (n + 1)\theta \sin^2 \tfrac{1}{2}\theta.$

According to the formula here presented, the life-curve for advanced ages bears no similarity to an asymptote, but ceases abruptly when the quantity $n\, k^n \theta = 90°$; or for the case of $k = 1$, when $n = \dfrac{90°}{\theta}$. This indicates that all ages above this limit are exceptional, and to be regarded in the same light as deviations from the theoretical number at other periods of life.

The many paths of research offered by the residual discordances from the formula must be passed by on this occasion, with the single remark that they offer indications of abundant reward for any explorer.

It is proper to add, that in these investigations, as in those on the Ages of Volunteers, the computations have been almost exclusively carried on by Mr. J. N. Stockwell.

CAMBRIDGE, January, 1866.

*280* *hart A.*

*4 year of age the relation*
*260 ed and computed numbers.*

represent the recorded numbers;
*240* are computed. Those for officers
, for greater distinctness.)

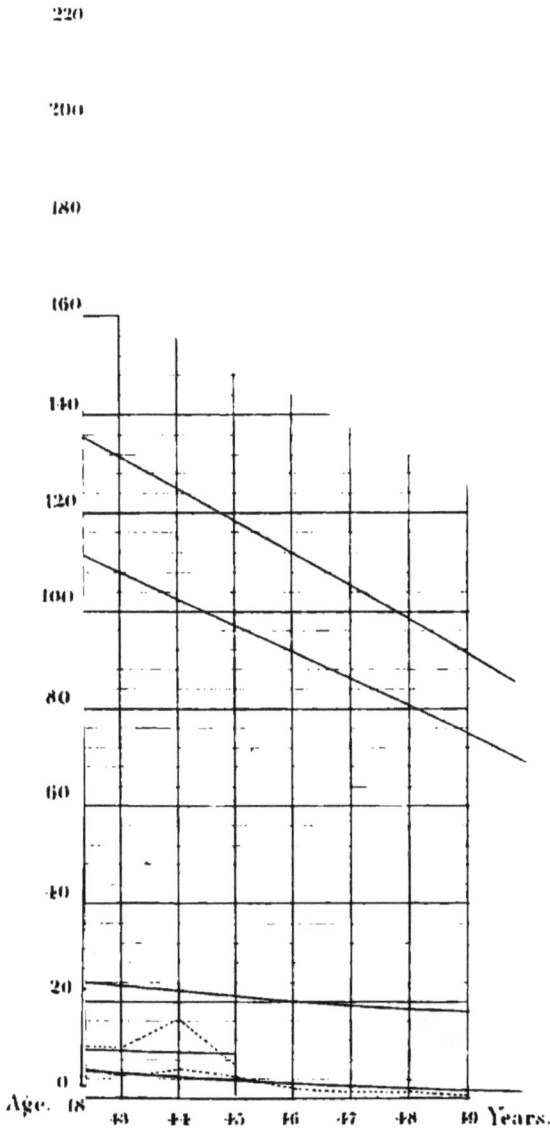

220

200

180

160

140

120

100

80

60

40

20

0

Age. 18    43    44    45    46    47    48    49 Years.

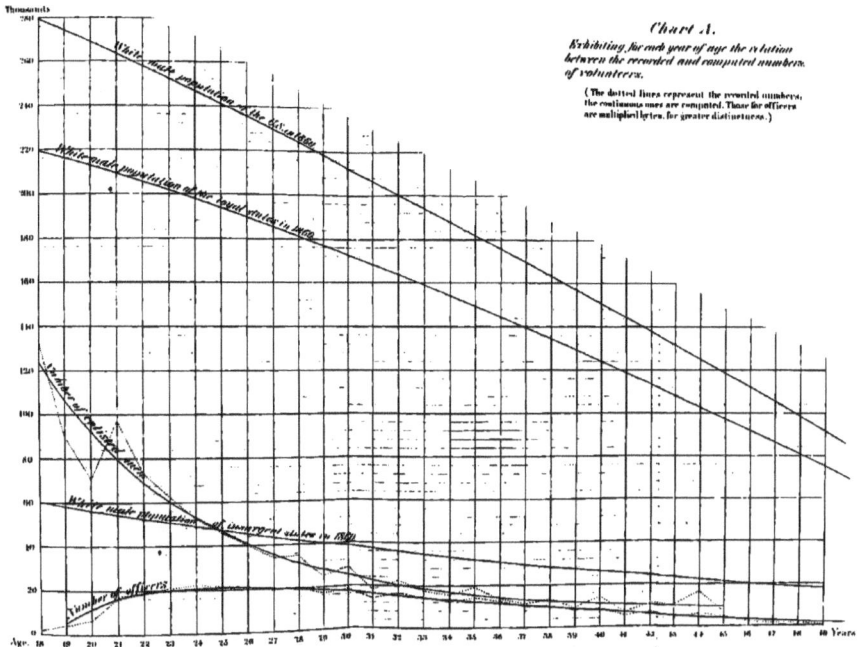

Chart A.

*Exhibiting, for each year of age the relation between the recorded and computed numbers of volunteers.*

( The dotted lines represent the recorded numbers, the continuous ones are computed. Those for officers are multiplied lยten, for greater distinctness.)

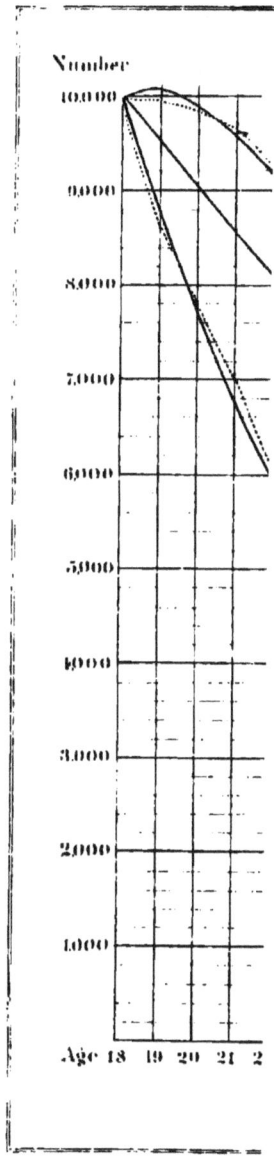

Number

10,000

9,000

8,000

7,000

6,000

5,000

4,000

3,000

2,000

1,000

Age 18   19   20   21   2

Number

10,000

9,000

8,000

7,000

6,000

5,000

4,000

3,000

2,000

1,000

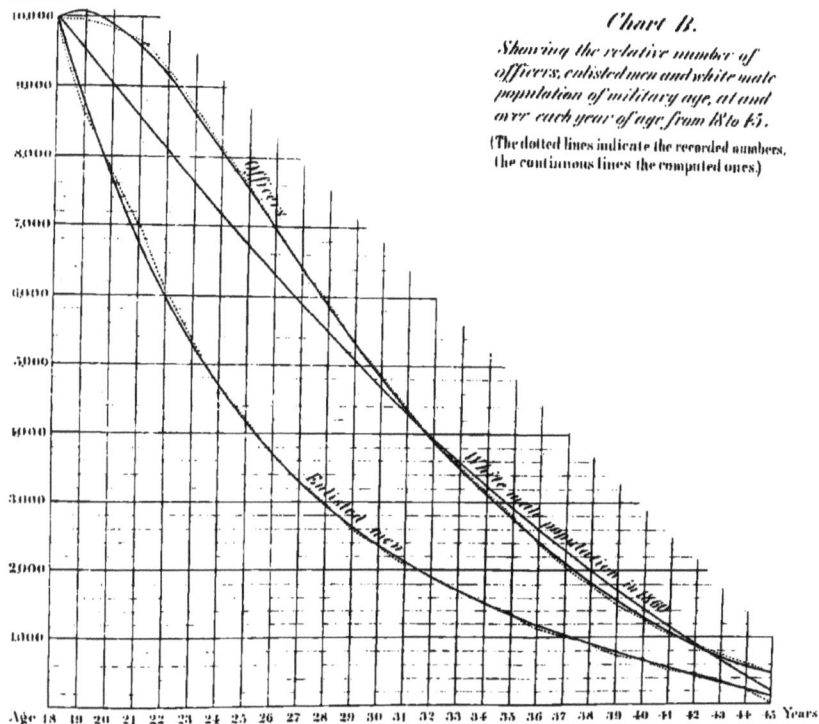

Chart B.

*Showing the relative number of
officers, enlisted men and white male
population of military age, at and
over each year of age, from 18 to 45.*

(The dotted lines indicate the recorded numbers,
the continuous lines the computed ones.)

Officers

Enlisted men

White male population in 1860

Age 18  19  20  21  22  23  24  25  26  27  28  29  30  31  32  33  34  35  36  37  38  39  40  41  42  43  44  45  Years

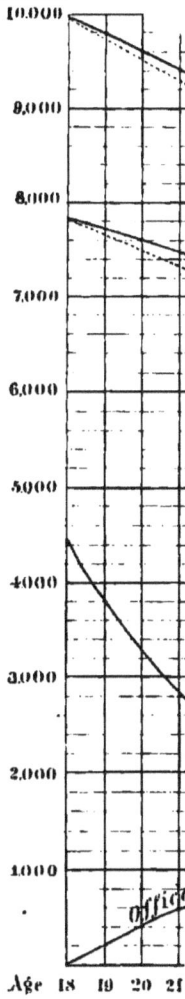

Number
10.000
9,000
8,000
7,000
6,000
5,000
4,000
3,000
2,000
1,000

office

Age   18   19   20   21

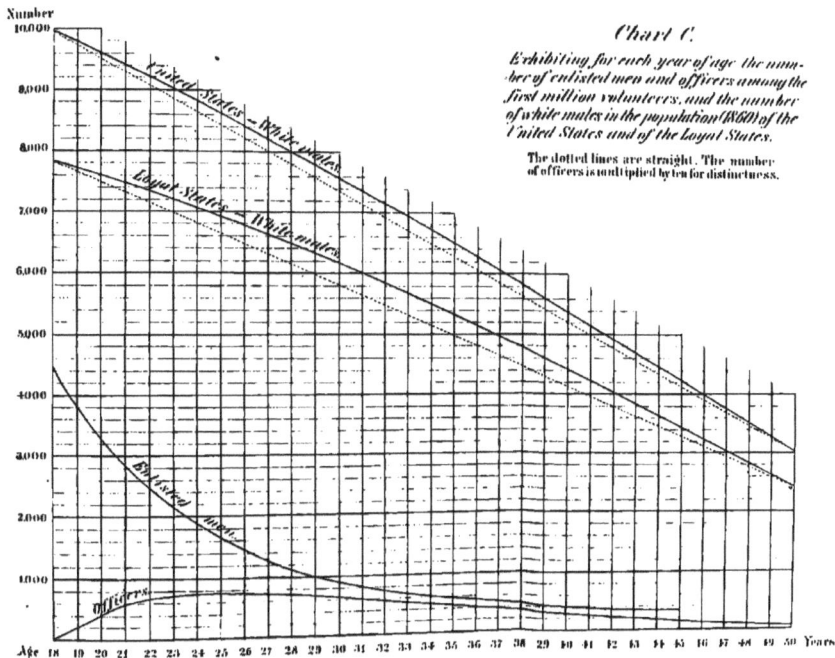

**Chart C.**

Exhibiting for each year of age the number of enlisted men and officers among the first million volunteers, and the number of white males in the population (1860) of the United States and of the Loyal States.

The dotted lines are straight. The number of officers is multiplied by ten for distinctness.

·

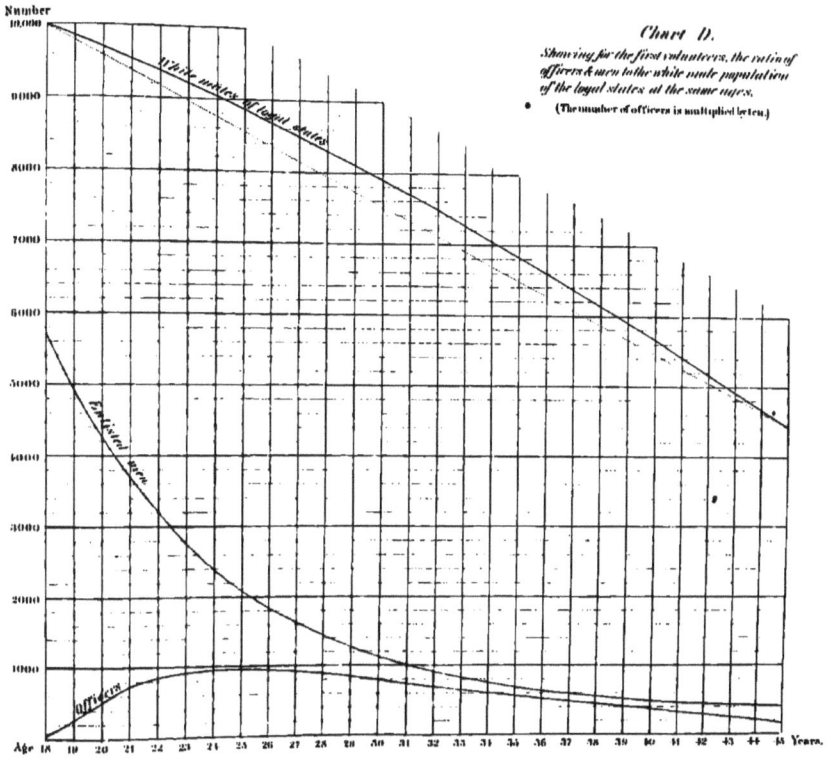

Chart D.

Showing for the first volunteers, the ratio of officers & men to the white male population of the loyal states at the same ages.

(The number of officers is multiplied by ten.)

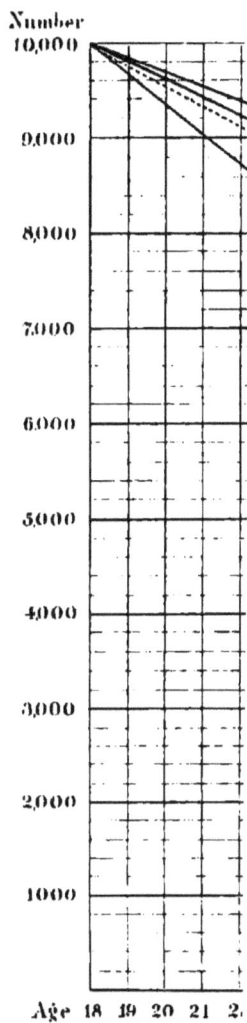

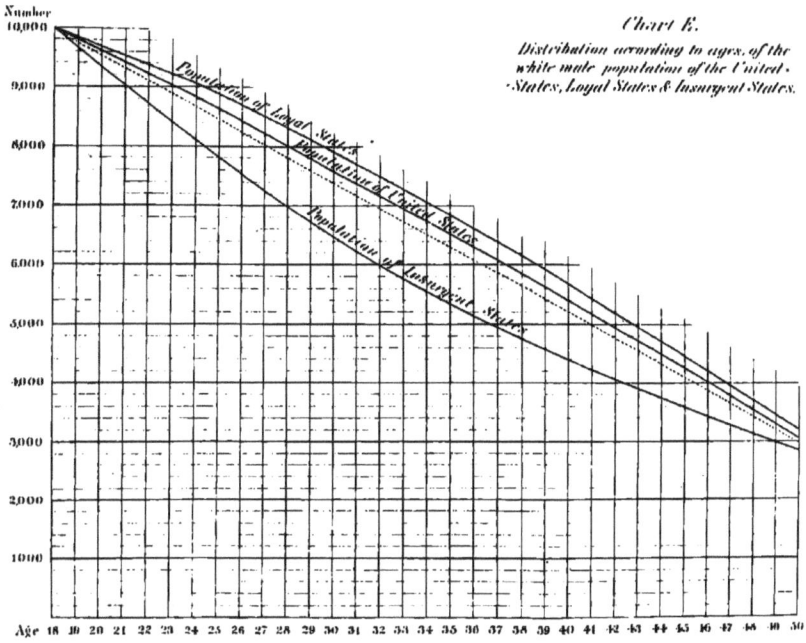

Chart E.

Distribution according to ages, of the white male population of the United States, Loyal States & Insurgent States.

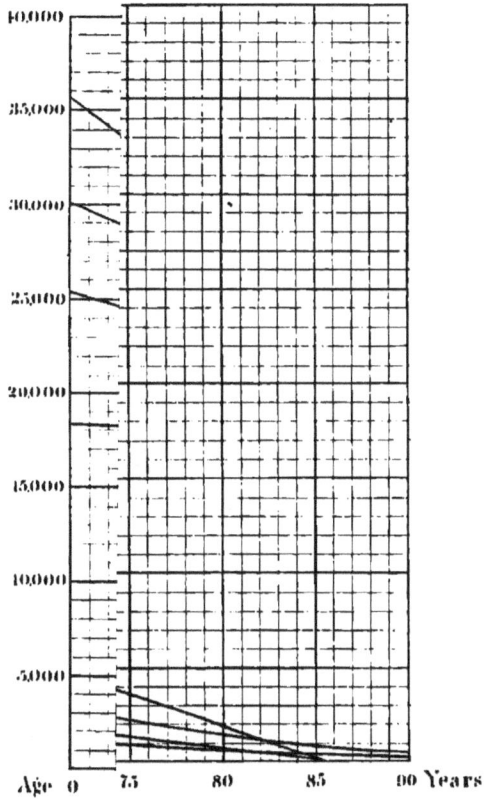

Number

40,000

35,000

30,000

25,000

20,000

15,000

10,000

5,000

Age  0        75        80        85        90 Years

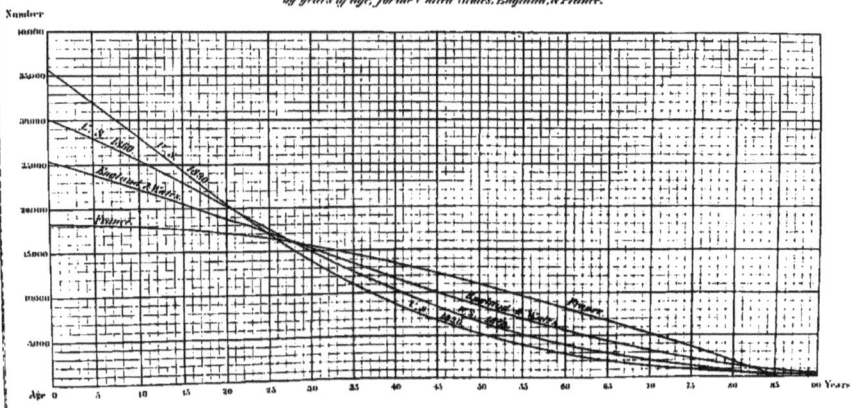

Chart F.
Shewing the distribution of a million of population,
by years of age, for the United States, England, & France.

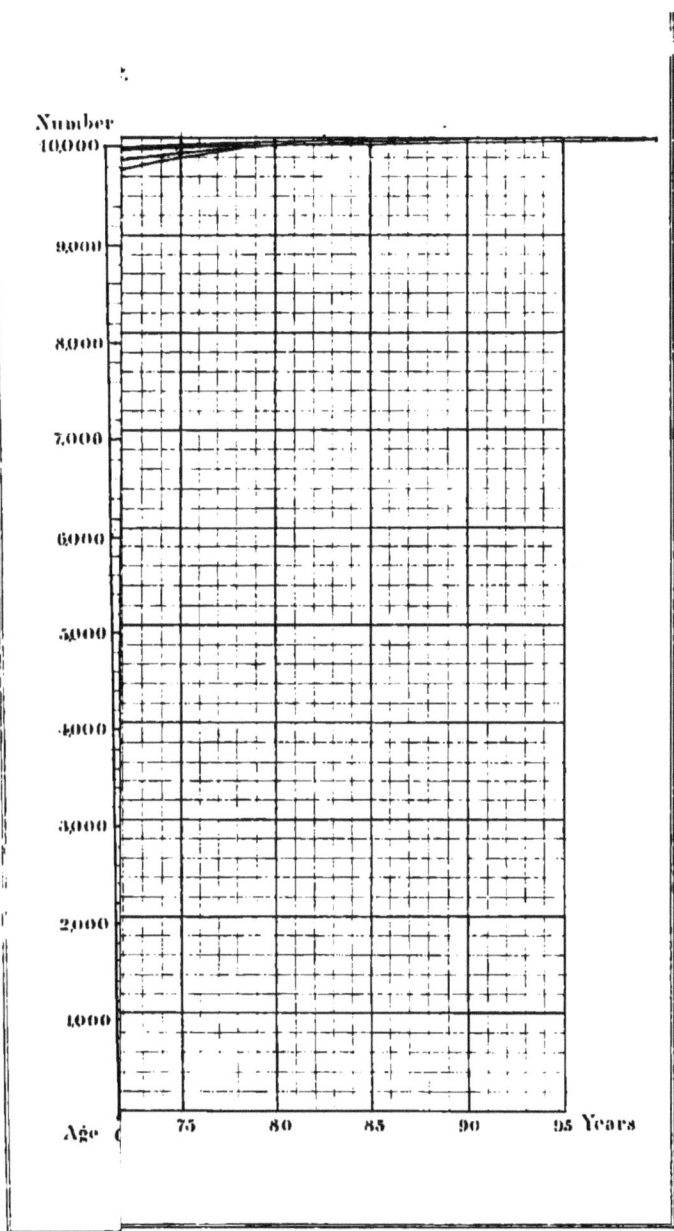

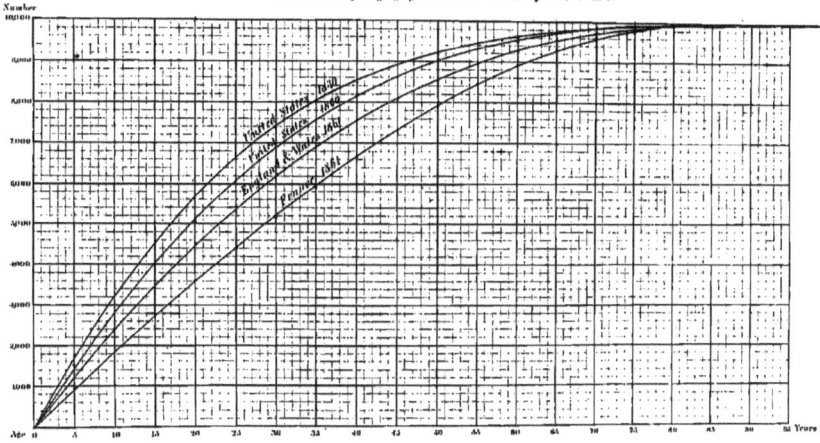

Chart G.

Exhibiting the relative number of the population under
each successive year of age, for the United States, England, & France.